# The West's War Against
# Islamic State

# The West's War Against Islamic State

## Operation Inherent Resolve in Syria and Iraq

Andrew Mumford

**I.B. TAURIS**

LONDON • NEW YORK • OXFORD • NEW DELHI • SYDNEY

I.B. TAURIS
Bloomsbury Publishing Plc
50 Bedford Square, London, WC1B 3DP, UK
1385 Broadway, New York, NY 10018, USA
29 Earlsfort Terrace, Dublin 2, Ireland

BLOOMSBURY, I.B. TAURIS and the I.B. Tauris logo are trademarks of
Bloomsbury Publishing Plc

First published in Great Britain 2021
Reprinted 2021

Cover design by Holly Bell

A catalogue record for this book is available from the British Library.

A catalog record for this book is available from the Library of Congress.

ISBN:   HB:     978-1-7883-1732-0
        PB:     978-1-7883-1733-7
        ePDF:   978-1-7867-3618-5
        eBook:  978-1-7867-2612-4

Typeset by RefineCatch Limited, Bungay, Suffolk
Printed and bound in Great Britain

To find out more about our authors and books visit www.bloomsbury.com
and sign up for our newsletters

*For Aurelia*

# Contents

# Acknowledgements

One of the joys of academic life is seeing a project morph over time. I never intended to write a book about Operation Inherent Resolve. I wanted to develop my previous work on proxy war by exploring in greater detail how the US and its allies after 2014 had decided to fight ISIS vicariously through a network of proxies. But it soon became clear that the indirect approach to degrading ISIS was only part of a wider story that involved limited kinetic action via an air campaign, pockets of special forces teams on the ground, and a web of cyber operatives trying to limit ISIS's online potency – all against the backdrop of contending interventions by rival powers including Russia and Iran. What started out as a short article gestated into the short book in your hands today. My sincere thanks go to Tomasz Hoskins, my editor at IB Tauris, for encouraging me to chronicle this war more holistically.

As always my colleagues in the School of Politics and International Relations at the University of Nottingham, especially those affiliated to our Centre for Conflict, Security and Terrorism (CST), have proven to be a superb sounding board for the ideas and arguments you will read in this book. I am immensely grateful to the many students who have taken my 'Contemporary Warfare' postgraduate class who, since 2014, have incisively discussed the implications of the rise of ISIS and the Western response with me. Omissions and errors of course remain squarely with me.

I would also like to thank my fellow panellists and audience members for feedback on previous iterations of some of the material in these chapters, especially at the 2018 European International Studies Association conference in Prague and the 2019 Society for Terrorism Research conference in Oslo.

I remain permanently indebted to my wonderful family for their support and inspiration – my wife Hannah and our daughters Elodie and Aurelia, to whom this book is dedicated.

# Introduction

Amidst the chaos of the withdrawal of American combat troops from Iraq in 2011, the insurgent group al-Qaeda in Iraq (AQI) morphed into the Islamic State of Iraq and Syria (ISIS). Having used its paramilitary force to take control of territory across both nations in the subsequent years, ISIS declared the foundation of a 'caliphate' stretching across 423 miles of Iraq and Syria on 29 June 2014. In response, a 74-nation Global Coalition was formed in September of that year. This coalition became the umbrella organisation that would support the US-led Combined Joint Task Force – Operation Inherent Resolve (CJTF-OIR), established in October 2014 to co-ordinate the multi-national response to the ISIS threat. This book is an initial attempt at understanding the conduct and consequences of that response.

At its zenith in 2015, ISIS governed over 11 million people with an income equivalent to the gross domestic product of Liechtenstein.[1] But the Iraqi and Syrian militaries, along with an alphabet soup of local militias being used as proxy ground forces by the West, forced a constriction of the territory under ISIS control by retaking key cities. ISIS underwent a 23% reduction of its territorial space in 2016 (leaving 60,400 km² under its control[2]), down to just 20 km² left by the end of 2018[3] – a loss equivalent to going from the landmass of the United Kingdom to that of downtown Manhattan. This book will trace how Operation Inherent Resolve facilitated this decline, and assess how the strategic imbalance between coalition provision of air power and train-and-assist missions compared to the ground war fought by proxies in various militia groups.

Methodologically this study is empirical and inductive, utilising an extensive amount of authoritative open-source primary and secondary material to make a short contribution to the first draft of history written about the war against ISIS. In many ways the book represents an unofficial campaign history of Operation Inherent Resolve, breaking down the operational components of the anti-ISIS fight into separate chapters in order to build a comprehensive analytical assessment of the military effort (and its political management) to destroy the self-proclaimed caliphate of ISIS. Operational histories are not especially in vogue in war studies circles right now, but they are important as they offer a snapshot of contemporary strategic culture. Understanding Operation Inherent Resolve allows us to go some way towards understanding how, by the second decade of the twenty-first century, Western political perceptions of risk management had become ubiquitous. It reveals how the long shadow cast by the 2003 invasion of Iraq still hung over Western willingness to militarily engage in large-scale warfare with an irregular enemy. It reveals a strategic preference for a mix of limited kinetic action (lower-risk air strikes and an increasing reliance of Special Operations Forces [SOF]) and a dependence on proxies to take the fight to ISIS on the ground. The result was an uncomfortable strategic premise for Operation Inherent Resolve: defeat ISIS but without expending too much conventional force whilst displacing the highest kinetic risk to others.

It is worth quickly stating what this book will *not* be. It will not be a book that substantially reflects on the ideology, structure, or operational performance of ISIS itself. This has already been masterfully done by other authors with a specialist knowledge of Islamist terrorism.[4] It will also not be a book about domestic counter-terrorism responses to ISIS-affiliated 'lone wolves', sleeper cells, or returning foreign fighters. Again, this has been done elsewhere by subject area specialists.[5] Instead, this book will focus on the political effort and military campaign to roll up ISIS territory inside Iraq and

Syria, from the inception of the group in 2014, through the fall of Raqqa that marked the territorial collapse of the caliphate in 2017, to the withdrawal of American forces from Syria by President Trump in 2019. It should also be noted that throughout this book the label 'ISIS' will be used. Although the group formally changed its name to simply the Islamic State in 2014, the diverse nomenclature that pervades the literature on the group (ISIS, IS, ISIL, Daesh) has been made uniform in the name of simplicity.

There are a plethora of books on the US (and coalition partner) wars in Afghanistan[6] and Iraq[7] from the George W. Bush-era 'War on Terror'. But there is a lack of literature assessing the most recent iteration of the Western fight against terrorism in the Middle East. The absence of American combat troop 'boots on the ground' has perhaps made the topic a little less appealing to historians of modern wars, but collectively the story of the air war, proxy alliances, SOF, and cyber component of the war against ISIS needs to be told.

The West adopted a two-pronged strategy against ISIS: direct intervention in the form of limited airstrikes and targeted SOF missions, augmented by indirect intervention in the form of sponsoring proxy militias on the ground. In September 2014 President Obama outlined the essential duopoly of this approach, arguing that it would take time to 'make sure that we have allies on the ground in combination with the airstrikes that we've already conducted'.[8] This book will lay out the difficulty that Western military commanders and political leaders had in balancing these components. It argues that two key, intertwined weaknesses fundamentally undermined Operation Inherent Resolve. The first weakness was a lack of a political vision for post-ISIS Syria. Bashar al-Assad still remains in Damascus, even if ISIS has been largely purged. The fate of this leader and that group are inextricably linked. As this book will show, the West's response to Assad's actions during the Syrian civil war which began in 2011 coloured their actions in relation to the rise of ISIS in 2014. Assad's astute self-characterisation as a lynchpin in the war against ISIS transformed him into a de facto ally and ultimately preserved his own regime – but at the price of the West being unable to offer an effective counter-narrative to the Syrian people living under the control of ISIS. The second weakness was the fact that the ghost of Operation Iraqi Freedom roamed Banquo-like through the corridors of Operation Inherent Resolve policy planning. The massive blowback resulting from the removal of Saddam Hussein – the creation of a huge security vacuum in which jihadist groups could proliferate – caused a quantum shift in opinion in Washington, and the West more widely, that regime-changing wars that put large numbers of Western troops in Middle Eastern countries were politically disastrous, financially unviable, and militarily unrewarding. Assad got to stay precisely because Saddam had gone. A major legacy of the Iraq War has been an intrinsic aversion – clearly fostered in the politically diverse figures of both Barack Obama and Donald Trump – towards large-scale military interventions that would be costly in blood and treasure. The dilemma facing the West with the rise of ISIS was therefore: how do we attain the objective of minimising our exposure to risk whilst simultaneously reducing the threat of the group? The result was a strategy that offered leadership but not ownership of the problem. It was a strategy that did not adequately reflect on the consequences of previous military interventions on states affected by ISIS (including Iraq and Libya) as well as the failure to adequately address the underlying context of the on-going civil wars in others (namely Syria and Yemen).[9] It was a strategy that conceived of ISIS in an isolated bubble – a hermitically-sealed problem that could be dealt with independently of any other wider political or conflict context.

Unsurprisingly, a strategy based on political compromise has ultimately only produced partial success. ISIS has been degraded but not destroyed. The self-declared caliphate may have been rolled up, but the threat from the group will evolve, be it through inspiring affiliates to attack targets in the West or through territorial expansion in its *wilayets* (provinces) where it established a presence in at least nine countries since 2014.[10] This is in part a reflection of a counter-strategy that was never truly designed to be capable of destroying ISIS given the mitigation of risk adhered to by leading members of the coalition. When assessing the strategic outcome of Operation Inherent Resolve, much of the explanation lies in understanding its strategic design. This was a campaign built around minimal kinetic exposure in the hope of gaining maximum possible effect via proxy forces. It also owes as much to ISIS's own internal deficiencies and tactical errors as it does to any stroke of coalition strategic genius.

## Structure of the book

The book starts by tracing the lineage of ISIS, from its genesis in the wake of the American invasion of Iraq, through to its manipulation of the chaos caused by the outbreak of the Syrian civil war. Chapter 1 also picks apart the ideological underpinnings of the group and attempts to reconcile their beliefs with their military action and state-building activities. It also evaluates the origins of the multi-national Global Coalition that was created with the strategic objective to defeat ISIS. The five 'lines of effort' that guided Operation Inherent Resolve will be assessed in order to interpret the levels of success the war against ISIS has met with.

In many ways Operation Inherent Resolve was an American mission with minor help from allies. Chapter 2 charts the course of US policy towards ISIS from Barack Obama's initial dismissal of the group as a 'jayvee team' of amateurs to Donald Trump's startling announcement of ISIS's apparent 'defeat' precipitating an American withdrawal. It argues that under both presidents American strategy lacked clear or credible objective. The US wanted to lead the charge against ISIS but was unwilling to expend too much political capital or

American lives. The result was strategic inertia and half-hearted leadership of the campaign.

The main heavy lifting done in the kinetic fight against ISIS was undertaken by an amalgam of different militia groups that the West came to rely on once it became clear that no ground war of their own would take place. Chapter 3 chronicles this hugely important *indirect* war against ISIS, as the US launched different, and eventually competing, funding programmes for various proxy groups. It also takes account of the parallel proxy war to remove Bashar al-Assad that affected the dynamic of proxy assistance to the counter-ISIS fight. The dangers of outsourcing war to proxies are also assessed, especially the medium-to-long-term 'blowback' that can be expected from implementing a poorly managed programme of weapons provision.

Chapter 4 evaluates the collective legacy of the ground and aerial strands of the campaign, namely the air war against ISIS (including airstrikes on units of fighters and drone strikes on 'high value' leadership targets); the utility of SOF missions (including hostage rescue raids); and the 'train, advise, and assist' mission of local forces inside Iraq. These three elements are tied together by virtue of the fact that they offered the Global Coalition a way out of launching a major ground offensive. Investing heavy political belief in the application of comparatively lower-risk bombing campaigns and surgical strikes with small SOF teams, the coalition could claim to be taking the fight to ISIS without having to commit to a conventional 'boots on the ground' deployment. The training of Iraqi military personnel, something that had been on-going for a decade previously, was also a convenient way of deflecting the kinetic onus of retaking territory held by ISIS. Softened up by coalition airstrikes or SOF teams, the villages, towns, and cities under ISIS control would ultimately be liberated by a combination of state military forces (in Iraq and Syria) and affiliated proxy groups. This was the uneasy foundation on which the coalition's strategy would rest.

As Leon Trotsky nearly said, you may not be interested in cyber war but cyber war is interested in you. Although ISIS proved to be effective manipulators of the digital space to spread their propaganda and garner new recruits, the coalition proved remarkably slow in responding to the 'virtual caliphate'. Chapter 5 explores how ISIS used cyberspace and investigates the eventual counter-measures that were undertaken. It also analyses another crucial, but often overlooked, component of the campaign, namely the counter-finance initiatives that were applied. Restricting the flow of ISIS funding was one of the coalition's five 'lines of effort' against the group, and this chapter reveals how it was actually military action that proved more effective at reducing ISIS's financial resources than orthodox counter-financing initiatives involving asset-freezing.

An important strand of the book will be to evaluate the impact that the rival military interventions undertaken by Russia, Iran, and Turkey inside Syria and Iraq had on Operation Inherent Resolve. Contending regional powers undoubtedly complicated the political sensitivities of authorising airstrikes on certain militia groups who were receiving backing from non-Western governments. Operation Inherent Resolve was not conducted in splendid isolation. Chapter 6 will trace how its strategic objectives and operational design were hampered by rival powers trying to engineer their own outcomes in the war against ISIS and helps us understand how the coalition was politically outmanoeuvred by this alternative power axis.

The concluding chapter of the book explores how President Trump's talk of 'defeating' ISIS has seriously skewed expectations about the future potency of the group. ISIS is not defeated, just degraded. The war against them is over only in its current iteration. Future operations against new pockets of ISIS territory in areas farther afield than Syria and Iraq are highly likely. The group is engaged in a period of enforced organisational and strategic adaptation, due to both its territorial losses and the death of its leader Abu Bakr al-Baghdadi. The outbreak of the COVID-19 pandemic has brought an abrupt end to Operation Inherent Resolve training missions, but it has also afforded ISIS breathing space to recalibrate. The West's war against the caliphate may be over, but the war against the *wilayets* will be a future round of the Forever War.

# 1

# The Rise of ISIS and the Creation of the Coalition

## The invasion of Iraq, the Syrian civil war, and the rise of ISIS

The rise of ISIS has its roots in the creation of al-Qaeda in Iraq (AQI) after the American invasion of that country in 2003. Depicted by the Bush administration as a core plank of the 'War on Terror', the removal of Saddam Hussein turned Iraq into a global magnet for jihadists, creating a hotbed of extremism where it had previous not existed. AQI was initially led by the Jordanian Abu Musab al-Zarqawi who, until his death in an American airstrike in June 2006, had become a hugely significant figure in modern jihadism. His embrace of increasingly brutal tactics (pioneering the use of hostage murder videos released on the internet) and overt targeting of Shia Muslims over Western coalition soldiers marked an open break with the al-Qaeda core leaders Osama bin Laden and Ayman al-Zawahiri (in hiding since the 9/11 attacks).[1] The fledgling leadership of ISIS was forged in the American detention facility at Camp Bucca in Iraq, where AQI suspects – including the PhD-toting theologian Abu Bakr al-Baghdadi – were allowed to mingle, plotting a future iteration of jihad in Iraq and the wider region. Stewing in ever increasing amounts of anti-Americanism, these detainees featured several high-profile members of Saddam Hussein's old Ba'ath party regime, including Abu Ali al-Anbari and Abu Muslim al-Turkmani, as well as foreign jihadists like the Chechen fighter Omar al-Shishani.[2]

Yet its transformation into the fighting force that threatened to reshape the Middle East owes more to the disorder created by the outbreak of the Syrian civil war than the invasion of Iraq. Bashar al-Assad took over the presidency of Syria after the death of his father in 2000. Protests against his rule spread across the country in 2011, mirroring other anti-authoritarian protests across the region as part of the so-called 'Arab Spring'. A heavy crackdown on these protests by Assad's pro-Shia Allawite regime ensued, entrenching sectarian tensions within the country. The protests turned increasingly violent, resulting in the creation of numerous armed militia groups who shared the common aim of overthrowing Assad. Ready to exploit the new civil war in Syria was the remnants of AQI, who had crossed the border after being pushed out of their Iraqi stronghold of Anbar province in 2007.

The effects of the spill-over from the 2011 Arab Spring provoked a profound reassessment of Western interpretations of the utility of force for a few key reasons. First, the impact of the fall (or attempted removal) of regimes like Colonel Qaddafi's in Libya or Bashar al-Assad's in Syria brought significant political changes in the Middle East region that have created complex, unresolved civil wars with large implications for neighbouring states. Second, the escalation of Syrian protests into full-scale civil strife conditioned the rise of ISIS and an effective security meltdown along the porous border with Iraq. Third, and most importantly, reconsideration of the use of irregular forces has come about in large part because of the contradictory demands created by the prosecution of proxy wars against both the despotic regimes and ISIS. Suddenly, as the political and strategic picture of the region shifted, rebels, guerrillas, militias, paramilitaries, insurgents, and auxiliaries all became useful to the West, in a process that immediately questioned traditional modes of alliance formation. This, as Chapter 3 will show, foregrounded the use of proxies in the response to the rise of ISIS.

AQI changed its name to the Islamic State of Iraq and Syria (ISIS) in 2012 to reflect their cross-border interests. Acting as a spearhead for extremist Sunni resistance to the Shia forces in charge in Damascus and Baghdad, ISIS fighters scored quick successes, rapidly gaining control of territory. So swift was their spread that they declared the foundation of a caliphate stretching across 423 miles of Iraq and Syria on 29 June 2014, with al-Baghdadi the nominated caliph. At its height ISIS contained around 40,000 fighters who had travelled from over 120 countries.[3] Using a combination of intimidation, guerrilla warfare, and more orthodox large-scale military assaults, ISIS proved capable of defeating national armies and rival insurgent factions. By September 2014, it 'was earning approximately $2 million per day, making it the wealthiest terrorist organization in the world.'[4]

## Understanding ISIS

The West's fears about ISIS were stoked by the strict adherence to the '"Prophetic methodology"' required of all those living under ISIS control. This created, in Graeme Wood's words, '"a dystopian alternative reality"' in which the group's millenarian agenda was ruthlessly enforced.[5] Despite such fear, the West misunderstood ISIS in two key ways, argued Wood. First was a tendency to lump ISIS and al-Qaeda together into a monolithic jihadist bloc which overlooked key differences between the two groups. Second was a reluctance to acknowledge ISIS's medieval religious premise which acted as the source of the group's worldview. Such misinterpretations arguably led the West to seek Shia proxies that were broadly anti-jihadist and/or exuded discernible nationalist qualities. This all means that one of the hardest (and long-term) components of the anti-ISIS fights will not be the kinetic battle to kill or capture ISIS fighters and permanently prevent their regaining of territory, but the securing of

Sunni acquiescence, in Iraq especially, for a non-extremist central government.[6] Therefore, the war against ISIS was as much an ideational one as it is a kinetic one.[7]

ISIS was, and still is, an amalgam of beliefs, actions, and agendas. As James Fromson and Steven Simon have argued, the group had 'four principal manifestations: a guerrilla army, Sunni revanchist political movement, millenarian Islamist cult, and ruthless administrator of territory'.[8] Taking advantage of the fragile situation in post-invasion Iraq and post-Arab Spring Syria, ISIS sought to channel Sunni disillusion and offer a violent alternative to the existing body politic.[9] At the heart of this approach was a desire to consolidate and then expand a territorial area for their self-proclaimed caliphate by underpinning classic tenets of state behaviour (monopoly of force, bureaucratic infrastructures, etc.) with ritual brutality, proselytisation, and guerrilla warfare.[10] Yet, as Colin Clarke points out, ISIS actually represented an aberration in the history of modern global jihadism.[11] Never before has a movement been so centralised, so well resourced, so widely supported, and so successful at establishing a physical territory it called its own. Craig Whiteside has even posited ISIS as the latest group to contribute to the lineage of insurgent organisations promulgating revolutionary warfare, stretching back to its Maoist origins in the mid-twentieth century, by dint of their application of an ideologically motivated political goal to a series of military operations with state-changing results.[12]

They quickly built the infrastructure of a pseudo-state using the administrative centres of Raqqa in Syria and Mosul in Iraq to regulate everything from motor vehicle licensing to birth certificates, from garbage collection to welfare payments, from police stations to sharia courts.[13] Consolidating this bureaucratic apparatus in the swathes of territory they held was an extremist millenarian ideology. This included the ethnic cleansing of Shias, minority groups like the Yazidis of northern Iraq, polytheists, and non-converting Christians, and the introduction of a well-regulated system of slavery.[14] It manifested a rigid patriarchal order that denied women their autonomy.[15] Strict rules regarding public behaviour were published in captured towns and cities, including bans on public smoking, the prohibition of alcohol and drugs, the compulsory veiling of women in public, and vigilante justice for homosexuals or perceived apostates.

## The creation of the Global Coalition

The establishment of the Global Coalition Against Daesh, to give it its formal title, was announced by President Obama on 10 September 2014, to offer political leadership to the military Combined Joint Task Force – Operation Inherent Resolve (CJTF-OIR), which had been launched on 8 August with the motto 'One Mission, Many Nations'. The Global Coalition had actually been informally launched at the NATO Summit in Newport, Wales earlier in September, where NATO leaders had agreed 'that there is no time to waste in building a broad international coalition' to take on ISIS.[16] Eventually 82 nations would join the coalition, but, as we shall see later, there was a huge variation in the ability and willingness of coalition members to contribute to the military campaign. Although there was no explicit legal basis for the coalition in terms of a UN Security Council Resolution, for example, the Obama administration stressed that military action against ISIS was covered under pre-existing authorisation for the use of military force (AUMF) agreements.[17] On 3 December 2014, the coalition announced its strategy against ISIS and delineated responsibility for coordinating five 'lines of effort': support military operations, capacity building and training (to be led by the US and Iraq); to stop the flow of foreign fighters (led by the Netherlands and Turkey); to cut off ISIS finances (led by Italy, Saudi Arabia, and the US); to tackle the humanitarian crises (led by Germany and the United Arab Emirates

[UAE]); and to ideologically delegitimise ISIS (led by the UAE, UK, and US).[18] As an indication of the military priorities of Operation Inherent Resolve, the military command of the Combined Joint Task Force enunciated a different set of 'lines of effort' to the political leadership of the Global Coalition. The three lines identified by the CJTF were: enable the military defeat of ISIS; enable sustainable military partner capacity; and leverage cohesive coalition efforts.[19]

The military planners at CJTF-OIR designed the campaign around the standard four phases: Phase I was the noted 'Degrade' period in which the coalition would retard ISIS's continuing expansion; Phase II focused on 'Counter-Attack', whereby coalition forces would actively work to liberate territory from ISIS; Phase III would nominally see the 'Defeat' of ISIS through 'decisive battles' and all pockets of resistance cleared; finally, Phase IV would 'Support Stabilization' through security and development provision to the Iraqi government and some unidentified 'appropriate authorities' in Syria.[20]

The first US special envoy to the Global Coalition, and thus its nominal leader, General John R. Allen, believed that the coalition's key objectives were: 'halting the terrorist group's forward momentum, empowering indigenous forces to be the final and lasting agents of the Islamic State's defeat, and coordinating much needed stabilization efforts'.[21] The first objective has arguably been met given the retaking of areas once under its control. Indeed, ISIS did not manage to mount a successful offensive operation since taking Ramadi and Palmyra in May 2015.[22] The second objective was an utter necessity given the absence of any desire by Western nations to undertake a 'boots on the ground' land invasion. The third objective is, however, worryingly unmet. By the end of 2017, the UN Development Program's Funding Facility for Stabilization (FFS) – the main funding mechanism to support reconstruction and civilian rehabilitation efforts in areas liberated from ISIS – was facing a $300 million shortfall in its finances.[23] Such long-term elements of the anti-ISIS strategy are at risk and could leave the door open for ISIS influence to return at a future date. In February 2018, in the wake of the liberation of Mosul, the coalition announced it was shifting the focus of military action against ISIS inside Iraq away from combat operations and towards stabilisation, including a new emphasis on building the capacity of the Iraqi military and police.[24] Six brigades of the Iraqi army, known as the Counterattack Brigades, had already been trained by the coalition and were instrumental in pushing ISIS out of Ramadi and Mosul.[25] However, such 'Iraqisation' of the on-going fight to maintain control of liberated territory needs to be matched with adequate funding otherwise 'stabilisation' simply becomes a by-word for hasty coalition exit.

It is worth pausing to reflect for a moment on *non*-membership of the Global Coalition. Note how Russia, China, Israel, and Iran did not become formal members – all of them important regional and global powers. It reveals the ulterior motives of some (especially in regard to their pre-existing relationship with the regime of Bashar al-Assad) but most importantly their absence left the coalition as a largely Western and Sunni Arab grouping, undermining the premise of a truly *global* coalition.

## The strains of coalition burden-sharing

Just over a year after the creation of the Global Coalition over 50 members, nearly three-quarters of the total, had not actively participated in airstrikes against ISIS, leaving a distinct perception that it was more of a political umbrella group than a body coordinating military operations. As a result, only 24 of the nations delivering the core objectives of the coalition participated in the quarterly coalition coordination meetings chaired by the Americans.[26] Such unequal burden-sharing within the Operation Inherent Resolve team left Washington immensely frustrated. In February 2016, US Defense

Secretary Ashton Carter lambasted coalition partners for not contributing enough resource to the military campaign, singling out Turkey, the Gulf States, and European countries.[27] After leaving office, Carter labelled the Gulf States 'fence-sitters' on the ISIS issue, who 'contributed relatively little beyond talk'.[28] Intra-coalition friction was never far from the surface, but such is the nature of multi-national war-fighting. The Americans had experienced frustration with coalition partners in previous campaigns, notably in Afghanistan and Iraq, where anger at the obvious risk aversion of other coalition partners had been palpable.[29] However, the Global Coalition Against Daesh, unlike NATO partners in Afghanistan or the so-called 'Coalition of the Willing' in Iraq, was notable for being made up primarily of non-combatant nations whose lip-service to the objectives of the campaign were not backed up by tangible contributions.

Seemingly the Global Coalition was only as strong as the sum of the parts it contained. Frequently there were strains when unilateral efforts within the coalition to fight ISIS created friction with other partners. One such example is that of Jordan. In February 2015, King Abdullah of Jordan visited Washington to persuade members of Congress to authorise the sale of advanced military hardware to aid his nation's fight against ISIS. The king was in a meeting with John McCain, chair of the Senate Armed Services Committee, on Capitol Hill when news broke that ISIS had burned alive Muath al-Kasasbeh, a captured Jordanian fighter pilot, and posted the video online. In a meeting in the White House later the same day King Abdullah berated President Obama for not doing enough to help Jordan fight ISIS – a country who, the king claimed, were 'flying two hundred percent more missions than all the other coalition members combined, apart from the United States'.[30]

Some members of the coalition required a little more *quid pro quo* than others before agreeing to join the campaign against ISIS. The Polish government, for example, wrung guarantees from the US that it would enhance its military presence in Poland as part of the rotation of NATO troops in the country before it eventually acquiesced, nearly two years after the initial American request, to send a military contingent to Iraq (containing just over 200 troops and four F-16 jets).[31] Warsaw's participation in the coalition was thus as much about balancing Russian influence as about tackling jihadism.

The disparate burden-sharing of the military effort within the coalition can be put down, according to one major study, primarily to national perceptions of the threat posed to them by returning foreign fighters and a desire to maintain strong relations with the US.[32] Indeed, the very fact that each coalition member state used different operational code names for military action against ISIS revealed a multi-national effort that had distinctly individual components: Operation Okra (Australia), Operation Desert Falcon (Belgium), Operation Impact (Canada), Operation Chammal (France), and Operation Shader (UK).

## Key coalition partners

Despite the creation of the coalition the battle against ISIS was frequently hamstrung, especially in the first 18 months of Operation Inherent Resolve, by a lack of collective weaponry and equipment, friction between the coalition allies regarding burden-sharing, and an insufficiency of kinetic effect.[33] Operation Inherent Resolve was a fundamentally American mission, so much of this frustration was felt in Washington. Yet other key members of the Global Coalition did make a noticeable contribution to certain operations. It is worth taking a look at the role played by the UK, Australia, and France in particular.

The UK took a circuitous route to its eventual strategy. In August 2013, the House of Commons voted against sanctioning the use of Royal Air Force (RAF) strikes over Syria, meaning that recourse to war by proxy appeared to be 'the only alternative to inaction'.[34] But even this proved difficult to prosecute. In December that year, the UK and the US suspended 'non-lethal' aid to the Free Syrian Army (FSA) – the favoured proxy group – after the group had undergone a series of territorial losses near the Syrian border with Turkey, leading to fears that Western aid would get in to the hands of the then al-Qaeda-affiliated al-Nusra Front.[35] But Britain found alternative platforms to contribute to the anti-ISIS fight. This included taking a leading role in the counter-ideology 'line of effort' within the coalition. This saw UK military personnel waging large-scale information operations in which government contractors set up de facto press offices for some of the rebel groups and helped them disseminate propaganda. This emphasis on helping mould the communications messaging of the proxies started after the initial parliamentary rejection of airstrikes and continued after a second vote approved them in December 2015. Costing over £2 million by mid-2016, this initiative was sourced from the government's Conflict, Stability and Security Fund, and provided a key plank in Britain's efforts to degrade ISIS.[36]

The failure of the government of David Cameron to secure parliamentary approval for UK participation in US-led bombing missions against the regime of Bashar al-Assad in August 2013, in the wake of chemical weapons attacks by his forces, led to a fragmentation of wider US-UK cooperation over the situation in Syria. Disenchantment at the British contribution to the anti-ISIS fight from 2014 also began to grow in Washington quickly after the fall of Mosul to ISIS in June that year. Cameron's government offered at first little more than a commitment to assist the Kurdish *Peshmerga*. Obama administration officials began to lament British foot-dragging. It was only in late September 2014 that the House of Commons approved restricted air missions over Iraq, not Syria. Soon afterwards the prime minister told President Obama that he could guarantee no increase in the British military presence in the fight against ISIS until after the outcome of the next general election, due in May 2015.[37] By early 2018, the UK still had a 1,400-strong military contingent in Iraq, involved in air operations and training local forces.[38]

In October 2014, the Australian prime minister, Tony Abbott, committed his country to the deployment of eight Royal Australian Air Force (RAAF) F/A-18F Super Hornets (although only six were eventually deployed) and a Special Operations Forces (SOF) team to Iraq to contribute to the coalition (in addition to the early warning and control aircraft already patrolling Iraqi skies).[39] By the time Abbott was ousted as prime minister by Malcolm Turnbull in September 2015, Australia had built its military presence to contain an Air Task Group (ATG) constituting 400 personnel as well as 250 SOF operatives and 300 military 'advisors'.[40] The Australian military contingent remained broadly the same under the new administration, with Canberra remaining staunch in its support for Washington's strategy. Days after ISIS affiliates killed 129 people in attacks across Paris in November 2015, the French government significantly stepped up the intensity of airstrikes that its planes were conducting against ISIS targets in Syria. President Francois Hollande promised the French people he would be 'unforgiving with the barbarians'.[41] This approach also involved a significant deployment of SOF teams, sent to Iraq and Syria to 'hunt and kill' around 1,700 French nationals who had joined ISIS. President Hollande and his successor, Emmanuel Macron, were content with trying to prevent further acts of domestic terrorism by undertaking more aggressive military action inside the boundaries of ISIS's caliphate as part of the Global Coalition.

## Conclusion

Responding to the millenarian ideology of ISIS that inspired brutal acts of individual violence and societal repression was never going to be easy. The general desire to 'do something' was stronger than the specific vision of what that something should be. Operation Inherent Resolve is symbolic of the coalition-based war-fighting approach that has now become representative of Western uses of force in the twenty-first century (building on the NATO-based mission in Afghanistan and the informal, albeit more controversial, 'Coalition of the Willing' in Iraq). There was a clear disparity of effort among coalition members, but this is as much a by-product of a lack of military engagement by many nations as it is the American desire to lead the war effort but not own it. The Global Coalition proved effective at stymying the eventual growth of ISIS and coordinated a military campaign that did help contribute to its territorial diminution, but it never offered a convincing political solution to the problems that sparked the group's rise in the first place. The coalition was caught up in the intractability of the enmeshed Syrian civil war, yet became overtly conscience of avoiding a repetition of the egregious mistakes of Operation Iraqi Freedom by engineering regime change or mass nation-building projects. Each member nation brought to the coalition its own particular domestic imperatives to want to act against the group, be it a desire to politically align more closely with Washington or enact a combination of retribution and deterrence against past and future terrorist attacks on their soil. The result was a fragmented strategic affair – a vehicle to purportedly 'defeat' ISIS made up of many moving parts, each not quite knowing what the other was doing, with only a vague sense of direction towards its final destination.

# 2

# America's War – From 'Degrade and Destroy' to the 'Defeat' of ISIS

Initial US policy essentially amounted to a containment strategy that relied on partner forces doing the fighting on the ground, supporting regional allies, and opting for limited airstrikes. But this strategy was hamstrung by the fact that the US was the only major intervening power who held the destruction of ISIS as its main strategic priority. Washington was outmanoeuvred by Russia, whose focus was on the survival of the Assad regime; by Iran, whose key objective was securing its own regional dominance; and even by fellow Global Coalition members, including Turkey, whose aim was to prevent the proliferation of Kurdish nationalism. The US may have led the coalition but the line they were towing had few influential followers.

A key weakness in US policy towards ISIS was the bifurcation of its strategy along territorial lines.[1] ISIS in Syria would be dealt with under the auspices of attempting to find a political compromise to end the civil war in that country (or, at the very least, hope that Assad and ISIS would degrade each other to the point of mutual destruction), whilst tackling ISIS in Iraq was given higher priority because of the desire to protect the new democracy that America had controversially fought hard to establish.

Yet the biggest weakness of all in the American strategy was the lack of a clear or credible strategic objective, allowing a gulf to emerge between expectations of what should, in theory, be done to 'degrade and destroy' ISIS and what, in practice, was achievable. As J.M. Berger put it, in the early years of Operation Inherent Resolve, the US did not so much have a coherent strategy as a loose collection of 'hopes and dreams ... tossed in a box labelled "strategy"'.[2] This was made all the more painfully obvious owing to the lucid realisation of a clear strategic plan by ISIS itself whose politico-military campaign to establish their caliphate was swiftly executed. Considering that the first three years of Operation Inherent Resolve cost the US over $14 billion (equating to a daily cost of $13.6 million[3]), American strategy reaped not a lot of bang for its buck.

## The battle to 'degrade and destroy' ISIS under Barack Obama

After the fall of Mosul in June 2014, a stunned White House authorised US air combat patrols, launched from US Navy carriers in the Gulf, to strike ISIS targets to prevent the group making further gains into Kirkuk and Baghdad later that summer.[4] Obama told a group of his national security team in August 2014 that he was 'aggravated' at the quality of information he was receiving about the spread of ISIS around Mosul. After the crisis on Mount Sinjar, where ISIS had corralled thousands of ethnic Yazidis and began perpetrating systematic human rights abuses, Obama's deputy national security advisor, Ben Rhodes, admitted that 'a sense of crisis enveloped the White House'.[5] This befuddled sense of crisis management spread into American handling of the proliferation of ISIS in Syria as well. Even some of the initial US air strikes inside that country in autumn 2014 were on groups like the al-Qaeda-affiliated al-Nusra Front, who had an antagonistic relationship with ISIS.[6] Strategic cohesion was lacking from the very outset.

There were hawks on Capitol Hill, noticeably senators John McCain and Lindsey Graham, who viewed the very emergence of ISIS as symbolic of the failures of American policy in the region in previous years.[7] Obama's withdrawal of combat troops from Iraq in 2011 and the decision not to decisively remove Bashar al-Assad from power at the start of the Syrian civil war were particular bones of contention. Though not to absolve Obama of a failure to construct a coherent initial response to the rise of ISIS, this hawkish logic goes too far. It overlooks the legacy of Bush-era foreign policy mistakes in the region – not least of which was the effective creation of a jihadist playground inside Iraq after 2003. Obama's desire to ameliorate the effects of this did, however, push him indelibly down a path of tentative engagement with the emergence of new regional threats like ISIS. Obama wanted to reverse the cause of American military action in recent years (a neo-conservative desire to forcibly spread democracy) but became blindsided by its effects (a growth in sub-state, jihadist threats regionally). One of Obama's main mistakes in his initial wave of thinking was to want to restrict US military action against ISIS in Iraq until Nouri al-Maliki had been replaced 'by a less sectarian leader.'[8] This reveals a preliminary desire to see ISIS mainly through the prism of Iraq and a cautious mind-set that wanted to wait for political fates to align in Baghdad, all whilst ISIS continued its ruthless conquest of territory, enslaving women and children, executing non-Muslims, and rigidly enforcing their code on occupied communities.

For critics of Obama's approach to tackling ISIS along the 'lines of effort' crafted by the Global Coalition, this represented only a partial strategic approach (the 'means') but was let down by the failure to settle on identifiable 'ends'. Alongside Obama's stated desire to 'degrade and destroy' ISIS, administration officials had simultaneously referred to the 'countering', 'diminishing', and 'containing' of ISIS.[9] Even Defense Secretary Ash Carter came to perceive the 'lines of effort' as 'a list, not a strategy'.[10] Compounding this strategic inertia was an initial information campaign that was, in the words of Anthony Cordesman, based on 'overambitious spin and largely meaningless daily strike statistics'.[11] The basic strategic narrative was never effectively enunciated from the start.

It may seem strange that the comic book world of *Batman* had an influence on the way Obama viewed ISIS and the threat it posed. Presidential advisors retold a story to *The Atlantic's* Jeffrey Goldberg in which Obama analogises the innovative destructiveness of ISIS to a scene from the 2008 *Batman* franchise movie 'The Dark Knight':

> 'There's a scene at the beginning in which the gang leaders of Gotham are meeting. These are men who had the city divided up. They were thugs, but there was a kind of order. Everyone had his turf. And then the Joker comes in and lights the whole city on fire. ISIL is the Joker. It has the capacity to set the whole region on fire. That's why we have to fight it.'[12]

From this Gotham-inspired realisation emerged a broad three-pronged approach to tackling Joker-esque terrorism: a reliance on armed drones to eliminate targets; extensive security assistance to partner forces in the Middle East; and a programme of widespread electronic surveillance.[13] All three elements were utilised in the war against ISIS – a combination largely fostered by Obama's reluctance to put large numbers of US 'boots on the ground'. Wary of the huge follies committed in Iraq by his predecessor George W. Bush, Obama was keen to shift the onus of US counter-terrorism policy away from regime-changing conflicts that forcibly enhance democracy, and instead address the underpinning causes of terrorist violence through rolling out a programme dedicated to countering violent extremism (CVE). Even when announcing the first round of limited airstrikes against ISIS in August 2014 to break the Sinjar crisis, where thousands of ethnic Yazidis were stranded on Mount Sinjar trying to escape ISIS ethnic cleansing, Obama struck a cautious note, promising that he would 'not allow the United States to be dragged into fighting another war in Iraq'.[14] For Obama, countering ISIS was done with one eye on Operation Iraqi Freedom. As a result, between 2014 and 2016, US policy was as much about not repeating past mistakes as it was about trying to mitigate future threats.

In an address to the nation on 10 September 2014, President Obama formally announced the creation of the Global Coalition and also, crucially, framed the objective to 'degrade, and ultimately destroy, ISIL through a comprehensive and sustained counter-terrorism strategy'.[15] Yet again Obama sounded like a president haunted by the ghosts of wars past: 'I want the American people to understand how this effort will be different from the wars in Iraq and Afghanistan. It will not involve American combat troops fighting on foreign soil'.[16] The eventual strategic reliance on air power and armed select proxies was a direct result of a political desire to avoid a re-run of Bush-era massive interventions-cum-occupations.

It took nearly a year after Obama launched the first haphazard airstrikes on ISIS – in response to significant territorial gains they had made in Iraq as well as the killing of US hostage James Foley – before his administration had a cohesive campaign plan. This was in part due to the work of Defense Secretary Ash Carter. Two days after taking office in February 2015, Carter convened what he (unwittingly) called a 'Team America' meeting at Camp Arifjan in Kuwait, which pulled together all US military commanders, diplomats, and civilian leaders involved in the war against ISIS. The purpose was to evaluate the coherence of their current strategy and determine its future direction. Carter admitted that the conclusion of the meeting was that 'the United States and its coalition partners lacks a comprehensive, achievable plan for success', as well as an acknowledgment of poor intelligence on ISIS, an ineffective information campaign, and an incoherent chain of command directing operations. Carter appreciated that the US 'took longer than we should have to get our act together', but pointed to the introduction of particular 'accelerants' to Operation Inherent Resolve in the second half of 2015 that helped change the course of the campaign in the coalition's favour – including more Special Operations Forces (SOF), enhanced air strikes, and closer cooperation with Kurdish fighters.[17]

In September 2015, the US reorganised its military command structure of Operation Inherent Resolve, consolidating air and ground operational command under a single leader, Lieutenant General Sean McFarland.[18] Defense Secretary Carter also consciously started to change the strategic language that framed the war effort, dropping reference to 'degrading' ISIS and instead insisting on its 'lasting defeat'. Yet even by his own admission, this lasting defeat 'required enabling local forces to reclaim territory from ISIS and hold it rather than attempting to substitute for them'.[19] In short, the defeat of ISIS would only be lasting if actors other than the US shouldered the predominant kinetic burden. This logic of a proxy war rooted in localism was enunciated by Carter in August 2015 when he stated: 'We can help them [Iraqi and Syrian opponents of ISIS]. We can enable them. We can train them. We can equip them. But we can't substitute for them because we don't live here … we can't keep them [ISIS] beaten. Only the people who live here can keep them beaten'.[20] This rationale for adopting a proxy war is fundamentally based on an assumption that large-scale external ground forces would not be forthcoming in order to beat ISIS in the short term, let alone undertake long-term security operations. Framing local actors as the only combatant capable of putting down a common enemy in the long run, laudable though that might be from a legitimacy standpoint, is still capable of excusing third-party combatants from shouldering a burden of the kinetic war-fighting. Simply, the Obama administration's strategy of working *by*, *with*, and *through* local partners was adopted because they wanted to work *against*, *without*, and *avoiding* large-scale troop deployments.

By the time Barack Obama handed the presidency over to Donald Trump ISIS had lost 43% of its territory.[21] Overall, it would be too harsh to accuse the Obama administration of doing too little too late – instead, it did just about enough too late. They coordinated a large multi-national response, which, mainly thanks to the arming and training of proxies on the ground, stemmed the tide of ISIS expansion before it reached Baghdad, but not before millions of people had been subjected to its rule and America's rivals in the Middle East, especially Iran, had positioned themselves as the saviours of Iraqis and Syrians.

## Donald Trump and the 'defeat' of ISIS

Despite President Trump's claims that his administration's approach to ISIS would be radically different from President Obama's, it is clear that there are far more continuities than differences between the two:[22] a reliance on air power, a reluctance to put in major combat forces, and an underlying assumption that this was not America's war to fight in the long run. These similarities have more to do, however, with the national security and military personnel surrounding Trump restraining the president's more impulsive tendencies. This continuity is despite, not because, of Donald Trump. Indeed, there was much actual continuity of senior military and diplomatic leadership in the campaign across the Obama and Trump presidencies. General Joseph Dunford remained Chairman of the Joint Chiefs of Staff, General Joseph Votel continued as commander of US Central Command (CENTCOM), General Stephen Townsend stayed in place as the Operation Inherent Resolve commander, and Brett McGurk continued in post as special envoy to the Global Coalition.

In the absence of anything as fixed as a discernible doctrine, Trump has at least demonstrated 'an instinctive aversion to anything that seems to throw dust in the eyes of America'.[23] Such an America First foreign policy has been evident in his handling of the ISIS campaign, where presidential tweets threatening use of force have been issued not out of a sense of obligation towards defending the liberal world order but out of a reflex action to respond to perceived slights to American prowess on the international scene. As with most other policy areas under the Trump presidency, the administration had *plans* for the war against ISIS but nothing that could be identified as a coherent *strategy*.[24]

Trump came into the Oval Office with a desire to largely delegate control of the war against ISIS to what he kept referring to simply as 'the generals'.[25] He was not keen to take a leading role in shaping policy. Yet key members of his inner circle were espousing some unorthodox opinions about how the war was being run. His chief strategist, Steve Bannon, for example, was spuriously claiming that Obama's national security advisor Susan Rice was 'running the campaign' and personally 'picking drone strikes'.[26] But even if Trump was not interested in the nuances of ISIS, they were interested in him. As journalist Mike Giglio reported from Mosul, where he had been in the months before and after Trump's election victory, ISIS online propaganda and clerical broadcasts from mosques were 'eager to show that Trump's rhetoric – from his call for a travel ban against Muslims to his promise that airstrikes he ordered against ISIS would pay far less heed to civilian harm – meant that ISIS had been right about America and its Western allies'. An ISIS defector told Giglio that ISIS leaders in Raqqa 'hailed Trump's win as divine intervention'.[27] His barely disguised Islamophobia had a rallying effect on ISIS.

In the same month he was inaugurated President Trump issued a memorandum outlining his administration's 'Plan to Defeat the Islamic State of Iraq and Syria'. This largely meaningless document really only contained an announcement that: 'Development of a new plan to defeat ISIS (the Plan) shall commence immediately'.[28] It took a year in office before the administration outlined a new set of objectives regarding the Syria crisis. In January 2018, Secretary of State Rex Tillerson laid out a five-point plan that focused on defeating ISIS in the long run through a long-term commitment of US military personnel and 'stabilising' a post-ISIS Syria, free from Iranian influence.[29] Tillerson acknowledged that: 'it is vital for the US to remain engaged in Syria ... [A] total withdrawal of American personnel at this time would restore Assad'.[30] Yet by the following year Tillerson was out and so was the logic of a continued US military presence in Syria.

On 18 December 2018, President Trump unexpectedly announced that ISIS was 'defeated' and therefore he was pulling all US forces – around 2,000 personnel – out of Syria.[31] Although Trump had been publicly mooting for a while his desire to bring US forces home, the timing of his announcement took many of his key officials by surprise. It smacked of a unilateral impulse by the president. Indeed, his announcement came just a month after Chairman of the Joint Chiefs, General Joseph Dunford, had stated that the US still had 'a long way to go' in the war against ISIS,[32] and just one week after the US Special Representative to the Global Coalition, Brett McGurk, had openly stated the need for long-term US commitment to Syria.[33] The announcement showed little heed to concerns over a potential return of ISIS in areas vacated by US troops, nor to the real likelihood of Russian or Iranian personnel filling the vacuum, thus ceding more influence to strategic rivals.

Trump's surprise announcement of a withdrawal of combat troops from areas formerly under ISIS control had several important consequences. First, it left erstwhile US allies, the Kurds, as a bereft bulwark against ISIS recidivism. A long-standing sense of betrayal, fostered by George H.W. Bush's failure to offer support to his incitement to the Kurds to rise-up against Saddam Hussein after the Gulf War, was compounded by Trump's clear lack of awareness at the sacrifices they had made in the war against ISIS.

Second, it indicated Trump's total lack of investment (or consultation) with Tillerson's original plan for a longer-term American presence – or indeed his own National Security Strategy, whose 2017 version had stated: 'The campaigns against ISIS and al-Qa'ida and their affiliates demonstrate that the United States will enable partners and sustain direct action campaigns to destroy terrorists and their sources of support'.[34]

Third, it symbolised a wider inchoate national security policy process within the administration, with presidential tweets out-strategising the policy planning process. Just three months before Trump's announcement, Defense Secretary James Mattis had bluntly stated in a Pentagon press briefing: 'Getting rid of the caliphate doesn't mean you then blindly say, "OK, we got rid of it", march out, and then wonder why the caliphate comes back'.[35] Even the head of CENTCOM, General Joseph Votel, admitted to the Senate Armed Services Committee in February 2019 that he 'was not consulted' by President Trump ahead of his withdrawal announcement.[36]

Fourth, it hugely undercut the multilateral coalition approach. This lack of consultation left the Global Coalition dangerously exposed as a team effort in name only. Trump's rhetoric of 'America First' came close to in fact meaning 'America Alone' as he unilaterally made decisions affecting the direction of a strategy that over 70 other nations had signed up to.

Fifth, it lost the president support within his own party inside Congress. Many Republicans on Capitol Hill openly questioned whether Trump had committed a perceived blunder equal to that of President Obama's 2011 withdrawal of combat forces from Iraq – a decision that, as mentioned earlier, senators like Lindsey Graham held to be the green light for the growth of ISIS.[37]

Confusion surrounding the Trump administration's ISIS policy pre-dated this hurried withdrawal announcement. The departure in quick succession of Secretary of State Tillerson and National Security Advisor H.R. McMaster in March 2018, led some US military commanders to privately vent their frustrations at an 'unfocused' White House. An 'operational pause' announced by Washington soon after those major personnel changes inside President Trump's national security team led one SOF commander to opine: 'We're on the two-yard line. We could literally fall into the end zone. We're that close to total victory, to wiping out the ISIS caliphate in Syria. We're that close and now it's coming apart'.[38]

However, it was the withdrawal announcement in December 2018 that triggered the unravelling of the administration's grasp of the war effort. The day after Trump's declaration of ISIS's defeat, Defense Secretary James Mattis resigned. After travelling to the White House to try and persuade the president that any withdrawal should be gradual, Mattis clearly felt that there were irreconcilable differences in worldview between him and his commander-in-chief, epitomised by what Mattis clearly believed to be a reckless abandonment of coalition allies, especially the Kurds, and American leadership in defeating ISIS. In his resignation letter Mattis pointedly wrote: 'While the US remains the indispensable nation in the free world, we cannot protect our interests or serve that role effectively without maintaining strong alliances and showing respect to those allies'.[39]

Sharing a similar frustration with Trump's view of a 'defeated' ISIS necessitating a troop pull-out was Brett McGurk. The day after Mattis resigned, the US special envoy to the Global Coalition announced that he too would be stepping down earlier than planned, telling colleagues in an email that Trump's plan 'was a complete reversal of policy that was articulated to us' and 'left our coalition partners confused and our fighting partners bewildered'. McGurk ultimately concluded that he 'could not carry out these new instructions and maintain my integrity'.[40] Trump's policy pivot cost him a Defense Secretary and a presidential envoy whose job was to keep the disparate Global Coalition united. By adopting a false equation of ISIS territorial losses to overall threat, Trump miscalculated the level of on-going assistance required to prevent any back-sliding on these hard fought gains.

The last shred of logic to American strategy was destroyed on 6 October 2019 when Trump pulled all US combat forces out of Syria, effectively green-lighting a Turkish invasion of the Kurdish areas of north-eastern Syria. President Erdoğan talked euphemistically about creating a 'buffer zone' on the Syrian side of the Turkish border to allow for the resettlement of Syrian refugees. However, only three days after US forces had followed presidential orders to leave their long-standing Kurdish allies in the Syrian Defence Force (SDF), the Turkish military launched an offensive against what they perceived to be Kurdish 'terrorists'.[41] Although Trump had to partially backtrack (largely due to pressure from inside the Republican Party in Congress) and threaten to impose harsh sanctions on Ankara if military action took place, the American abandonment of the Kurds is the most immediate legacy of Trump's exit strategy from the war against ISIS – followed closely by a Russian expansion to fill the security vacuum in its new mantle as regional power broker, as Chapter 6 will chronicle.

## Conclusion

For Donald Trump to imply that he judiciously expedited the demise of ISIS because the fall of Raqqa happened nine months after he took office would be the contemporary equivalent of giving Franklin Roosevelt no credit for winning the Second World War because final victory happened on Harry Truman's watch. In both cases there was more continuity than change in the American military action against the enemy. In US policy circles the conservative go-to counter-factual argument is that Obama's Iraq troop withdrawal in 2011 'created ISIS' by allowing a security vacuum to emerge that was soon filled by jihadist groups. The liberal counter-factual is that Trump's sudden withdrawal after his self-proclaimed 'defeat' of ISIS has let the group off the hook. As with most politically charged pieces of alternative history we must take each interpretation with a pinch of salt. Neither view is on solid ground. ISIS was already transforming its organisational outlook before Trump's announcement. Similarly, Obama bears distinctly less blame for the maelstrom of jihadi violence across Iraq than his predecessor George W. Bush, architect of the Iraq War. Yet the Obama administration's desire to avoid any repetition of Iraq War-style large ground invasions of Middle Eastern nations tipped their strategic calculus too far over into the realm of timidity in the face of the rise of ISIS. Their inability in 2014 to extricate the tackling of the ISIS threat from the larger, intractable problem of what to do about the Assad regime led to strategic paralysis at a crucial moment. The US strategy never truly recovered. That said, the Trumpian discourse of a 'defeated' ISIS is as dangerous as it is presumptive. The threat from the group is not eradicated – certainly not something that can be selectively ticked off a presidential 'to do' list and presented to voters as a major triumph in re-election year. The vacuum left by American disengagement will be felt most acutely, as it has since 2014, by proxy partners on the ground.

# The Proxy Wars For and Against ISIS

Proxy wars occur when third parties indirectly intervene in a pre-existing war in order to shape the outcome of that conflict in their favour.[1] This is the strategic logic that has underpinned much of the West's war against ISIS, with multiple militia groups, paramilitary organisations, and national governments all receiving indirect support in the form of weapons, money, and logistical assistance. With minimal 'boots on the ground' being offered by the coalition (beyond Special Operations Forces teams), the war against ISIS can predominantly be seen from a proxy war angle.

Since 2011 a myriad of foreign nations have been funding what has been labelled 'a chaotic melange of fighters'.[2] Syria was a particularly anarchic proxy war involving a broad network of shifting relationships between proxies and their benefactors, each with different goals in mind. The incredibly swift rise of ISIS, combined with their disregard for any other group or country, made strange bedfellows out of the resultant anti-ISIS coalition. America found itself united with Iran and other Gulf states in the effort to quell the rise of this virulent movement and roll back the borders of the self-proclaimed caliphate. The simultaneous battle to oust Assad from power in Damascus saw Turkey, Saudi Arabia, and Qatar channel financial assistance and weapons towards their favoured rival Sunni groups in the hope that it would lead to an outcome of their liking. Instead, this indirect interference was mirrored by pro-Assad Shia groups, like Hezbollah, being sponsored by Iran and Iraq. The result of this was that 'Saudi Arabia and Iran have been battling for regional supremacy – to the last Syrian'.[3] As one senior Iraqi politician noted of Tehran's use of proxy intervention: 'The Iranians have a PhD in this type of warfare'.[4] Beset by a disunited opposition and by a network of foreign intelligence agents, Syria became a particularly bloody proxy battle ground in which ISIS was not always the main target.

Stephen Saideman observed that 'there are two primary ways to participate' in the coalition effort against ISIS: conduct airstrikes or train forces on the ground.[5] This chapter suggests that there was a prevalent third option being taken by states: arm and finance militias to take the fight to ISIS by proxy. The mantra of 'my enemy's enemy is my friend' was the cornerstone of strategic planning for the proxy war against both the regime of Bashar al-Assad and ISIS. The two fights cannot be easily separated, but this chapter will identify why these instances of indirect intervention created the conditions for regional uprisings and insurgent violence across the Middle East to be infused with significant proxy activity. This chapter will evaluate the rise of ISIS and the opportunities for proxy war that it created, assess the ways in which proxy war manifest itself on top of the conflicts in Syria and Iraq, and highlight some of the strategic problems created by the prevalence of indirect intervention.

## The rise of ISIS and proxy opportunities

Proxy wars do not exist in isolation. They require a pre-existing conflict to create the conditions for third-party interference. Proxy wars, therefore, are always a second tier conflict layered on top of a different form of conflict, be it a civil war, an inter-state war, or an insurgency. To this extent, proxy wars are able to manifest indirect forms of intervention alongside direct modes of intervention, even by the same faction. This is the two-pronged strategy that the West adopted against ISIS and the regime of Bashar al-Assad: direct intervention in the form of limited airstrikes augmented by indirect intervention in the form of sponsoring proxy militias on the ground. In September 2014, President Obama outlined the essential duopoly of this approach at a press conference, arguing that it would take time to 'make sure that we have allies on the ground in combination with the airstrikes that we've already conducted.'[6] In other words, an indirect strategy will complement the direct strategy as soon as appropriate proxies could be secured.

Western perceptions of the appeal of an indirect intervention rubbed up against the strategic objectives of ISIS itself. The apocalyptic ideology of ISIS, based on Koranic predictions, confidently asserted that the caliphate would defeat the 'armies of Rome' in a grand battle.[7] If 'Rome' is synonymous with the West at large, then the prophecy is a long way from being fulfilled given 'Rome's' predisposition to arm, train, and fund local militias and militaries in the region and use them as proxies. To this end, no grand battle occurred because the West largely utilised third parties to take the fight to ISIS for them. But the assumption that proxies could deliver an overwhelming blow to ISIS and that an indirect strategy alone could stymie the organisation were overstated. As Will McCants pointed out, the multiple proxy war options on offer against ISIS contained multiple risks with marginal chances of success:

> Arming the Sunni tribes against the Islamic State doesn't guarantee they'll fight against it. They don't trust the Shi'i governments in Damascus and Baghdad and could just as easy decide to support the Islamic State or sit out the fight. Arming Arab Sunni rebel groups to fight the Islamic State is no guarantee they'll get the job done either. They're focussed on fighting their respective governments in Syria and Iraq and reluctant to tangle with a powerful rival . . . Arming the Kurds is attractive because they're more pluralistic, but they won't be able to do much against the Islamic State in its Sunni Arab stronghold.[8]

This was the proxy war dilemma facing the Western coalition. But the chimera of strategic success by proxy was a powerful one. During his term in office President Obama tried to resist this allure. Two months after ISIS declared its caliphate in 2014 Obama dismissed the notion that a more intense proxy war against the group would have stemmed its advance: 'This idea that we could provide some light arms or even more sophisticated arms to what was essentially an opposition made up of former doctors, farmers, pharmacists and so forth . . . was never on the cards'.[9] Yet this flippant dismissal of the proxy war option belies actions that he was forced to take in the subsequent years as the forces opposed to ISIS, especially inside Syria, shed their amateurism.

Collectively, the proxy warfare approach adopted by the West and Arab powers was a sign that they were trying to inflict death by a thousand cuts upon ISIS rather than inflicting a singular blow via a major land invasion. They had come to an assessment that a proxy war was, in the words of Tyrone Groh's book on the subject, the least bad option.[10] Yet it remains fundamental to the contours of the entire war effort that this approach was strategically compromised by the confusion over whether to prioritise the removal of Bashar al-Assad in Damascus as a prelude or a postscript to the defeat of ISIS.

## The proxy war against Bashar al-Assad

The proxy training of Syrian rebels to topple Assad began in 2012 when senior intelligence operatives from Qatar, Turkey, and Saudi Arabia established a 'military operations centre' on the outskirts of Istanbul. But in-fighting occurred in the management of this training camp as the benefactor states started to turn to different favoured rebel groups (especially hard-line Islamist ones) to achieve their aims at the expense of the West's favourite proxy, the Free Syrian Army (FSA), a loose coalition of 'moderate' anti-Assad fighters. As one Arab intelligence officer told *The Washington Post*: 'The Islamist groups got bigger and stronger, and the FSA day by day got weaker'.[11] This interpretation seriously undermined the West's backing of the FSA against Assad. The scale of such support was revealed by Saddam al-Jamal, a former FSA commander who defected to ISIS in 2013. He revealed to ISIS leaders that FSA military council meetings were attended by intelligence officials from Saudi Arabia, Qatar, the UAE, and, on occasion, America, Britain, and France.[12] But the FSA remained the preferred conduit for both the fading anti-Assad struggle and the nascent anti-ISIS one. Indeed, by March 2015 the British government were still putting their weight behind the FSA by authorising the deployment of 75 British military personnel to Turkey to help train FSA fighters in the use of light weapons and medical skills.[13]

In the summer of 2012, US Secretary of State Hillary Clinton encouraged CIA Director David Petraeus to compile a comprehensive plan that could 'train and equip' FSA rebels inside Syria who could topple Assad and act as a bulwark against ISIS. When presented to the president for consideration, Obama showed reticence at the idea of launching a proxy war, revealing fears at sparking another American imbroglio in a complex Middle East conflict. The right set of proxies, Obama insisted, had got to be found.[14] Yet by September 2013 he had be sufficiently convinced that a proxy war option was the only path of action he was willing to invest heavily in. It was widely reported in the US media that the CIA had initiated arms shipments to the FSA as part of a programme code-named *Timber Sycamore*, marking a distinct militarisation of America's proxy war in Syria. Approved groups under the FSA umbrella included the Syrian Revolutionaries Front (SRF), Liwa Forsan al-Haq, and Haraket Hazm. In April 2014, fighters from the latter group uploaded a video to YouTube showing them using American-made anti-tank missile systems – an event loaded with symbolism given how permission must have been granted from the US government for their provision.[15] By this point the CIA estimated that it had trained just shy of 1,000 fighters who could push the Syrian civil war to a point of stalemate (that could lead to a negotiated peace that would have seen the removal of Assad). Yet they were up against a rival proxy war effort to bolster Assad's position that saw Iran and Hezbollah train over 20,000 Shia proxies who attempted to nullify the effect of the Western-backed Sunni rebels.[16] This only increased Western reliance on the FSA to counter these efforts.

By September 2016, there were 78 different CIA-vetted factions of the FSA receiving American weapons and assistance.[17] Charles Lister has argued that this fragmentation of the once centralised FSA was in part caused by the absence of significant third-party support in the 12 months after its creation in 2011. In other words, the swift execution of a committed proxy war strategy by opponents of the Assad regime would have unified the anti-Assad forces under the FSA banner for longer, thus creating a singular channel for weapons provision and the potential for a more effective opposition movement. Instead, what had occurred by 2013 was the breakdown in the centralisation of the group and an increase in the autonomy of the multiple local Armed Opposition Groups (AOGs) that made up the FSA. This made it more difficult for the so-called 'Friends of Syria' group – the international coalition of Western and Middle Eastern countries established in 2012 – to coordinate proxy war efforts.[18] This highlights the problem of strategic diffusion for anti-Assad proxy war-wagers. The FSA became constitutive of too many groups vying for support, thus dispersing the channels for indirect intervention to be routed – and even then, funds to FSA fighters were too dispersed to make a difference. FSA members were paid between $100 and $150 per month. Crucially this was less than half the sum being offered by ISIS to new recruits. The lack of a financial allure to become a Western proxy was compounded by logistical difficulties too. One militia group leader revealed he could only dispense 16 bullets per month to his fighters. Amidst a wave of defections to ISIS, one commander told journalist Joby Warrick: 'We thought going with the Americans was going with the big guns. It was a losing bet'.[19]

The Obama administration's reluctance to act on the evidence that the president's self-drawn 'red line' on the use of chemical weapons by Assad had been crossed was arguably a sign that in regard to Syria, US policy had, in David Kilcullen's words, 'shifted from regime change to regime *behaviour* change'.[20] The rise of ISIS as a threat to regional security and not just the longevity of Assad's grip on power inside Syria was evident by the beginning of 2014. As an indicator of how the proxy battleground had shifted in Syria, even Assad himself was claiming that his own regime – so long the target of regional and Western indirect efforts – was actually being let inside the anti-ISIS tent by being offered 'information' on air strikes against ISIS targets inside Syria's borders.[21] So altered was the picture inside Syria in 2015 compared to 2011 that the proxy war effort that was once in place to overthrow Assad had recalibrated itself to stem the spread of ISIS, making Assad an uncomfortable but unacknowledged de facto ally in the process.[22] His regime, in the eyes of the West and many Arab capitals, was the lesser of two evils.

Assad himself has not been above using a proxy war approach to augment his own position in power. Assad's use of indirect interference in stoking jihadist violence in neighbouring Iraq pre-dates the rise of ISIS. Syrian assistance to foreign fighters crossing the border into Iraq began swiftly after the toppling of Saddam Hussein in 2003 and intensified during the first Battle of Fallujah the following year. Despite official denials from Damascus about helping orchestrate disorder in Iraq, former officials in Assad's government have indicated that Syrian sponsorship of jihadist violence, especially that of the nascent al-Qaeda in Iraq (AQI), was undertaken to simultaneously undermine the American military presence in Iraq as a means of dissuading Washington that further regime change in the region was necessary at the same time as deflecting jihadi attention away from his own position.[23] Yet the morphing of AQI into ISIS gradually broke the bonds of nominal influence between the group and

Damascus, even if they shared a common enemy. Between the start of the Syrian civil war in 2011 and the proclamation of the ISIS caliphate in 2014 it was widely appreciated that Assad and ISIS were 'tacit allies in a common war against the FSA'.[24] Even after ISIS began significant territorial expansion inside Syria in the second half of 2014 there were many within the Syrian regime itself that came to question the real extent to which Assad viewed ISIS as a convenient proxy in his battle to preserve his own regime from domestic rebels. Elia Samaan, a key figure in the Ministry of Reconciliation in Damascus, admitted that defeating ISIS was not a 'first priority' because Assad was 'happy to see ISIS killing' anti-regime fighters in the FSA.[25] The emergence of ISIS created further such strategic compromises within the West as a large-scale proxy war to counter the group got under way.

## The proxy war against ISIS

In June 2014, in the wake of the declaration of the self-proclaimed caliphate by ISIS, President Obama asked Congress to provide $500 million worth of training and equipment for 'appropriately vetted' Syrian opposition groups.[26] This represented a marked change of tune inside the White House. Earlier that year, Obama used an 'uncharacteristically flip analogy' when he likened ISIS to a junior varsity basketball team in the bigger league of jihadist groups.[27] The president and his team were slow to acknowledge the risk posed by ISIS but were quick to embrace a proxy war approach to tackling them after the caliphate was declared – an indirect approach that was arguably borne out of the legacy of the direct intervention in Iraq by his predecessor in 2003. The appetite for another land war in the Middle East was vastly diminished. An arms-length approach to fighting ISIS was thus adopted, creating a policy of 'shifting engagement' (as opposed to outright disengagement) in the region.[28]

A large step forward in the American proxy war against ISIS was taken in September 2014 when Congress passed House Joint Resolution 124, which legislated for the Pentagon to 'provide assistance to elements of the Syrian opposition and other Syrian groups for ... defending the Syrian people from attacks by the Islamic State ...'[29] Neither the specific nature of such assistance, nor the identity of the recipient groups, was detailed in the resolution, but it denoted a doubling-down on indirect efforts by Washington to use Syrian militias to dislodge ISIS from its strongholds. The following summer President Obama underlined America's commitment to proxy war by stating that in the absence of American forces 'an effective partner on the ground' would be necessary to sponsor so that 'ISIL can be pushed back'.[30] Yet deficiencies in the original 'train and assist' programme the president had announced a year earlier were now obvious. Not only were heavy losses inflicted on the American-backed militias, it was also clear that the number of graduates from American-run training camps in Jordan and Turkey was woefully low. US Central Command (CENTCOM) commander General Lloyd Austen was forced to admit to the Senate Armed Services Committee in September 2015 that only 'four or five' Syrian rebels were actively fighting ISIS having completed the training, despite an initial target of 5,000.[31] This prompted a revamp of the rebel assistance programme. The Pentagon committed to increasing the level of combat training that affiliated rebel groups received in the camps run by the CIA, as well as providing them with more intelligence and encouraging the groups to coalesce in larger numbers.

But US control over their proxies was tenuous at best. As Brigadier General Kevin J. Killea, the chief of staff of the US mission tackling ISIS, said at the outset of the relaunch: 'We don't have direct command and control with those forces once we do finish training and equipping them when we put them back into the fight.'[32] Not only was the US having quantitative problems finding numbers of recruits but qualitative ones in terms of securing ones that were still biddable to

American direction. Proxy selection in Syria needed to take into consideration not just their ability to kinetically resist and push back ISIS but also their ability to control and run the territory they retake – in other words, proxies that can 'fight *and* govern'.[33] This would have enhanced the effectiveness of the ground campaign to degrade ISIS whilst maintaining some legitimacy (and continuing American influence) over the post-ISIS situation. However, this balance was never truly attained. Symbolic of this was an incident in early 2016 when it emerged that two different Syrian proxies being sponsored by different agencies of the US government had turned their American-supplied weapons on each other. In a turn of events that came to epitomise the incoherence of the US anti-ISIS proxy war, skirmishes between the CIA-backed Furqa al-Sultan and the Pentagon-backed YPG (the Syrian branch of the Kurdish PKK) created the farcical situation of America fighting a proxy war against itself.[34]

But what is clear from Western action against ISIS is that proxy forces on the ground have been essential to the conduct of American-led Combined Arms Manoeuvres. Proxy forces helped contain ISIS fighters into limited territorial areas in order for Western airstrikes to be carried out with greater precision. Coalition Joint Terminal Attack Controllers (JTACs) would embed with the local forces in order to 'advise, assist, and accompany' the proxy forces in a training capacity. This simultaneous direct and indirect approach created a paradox in which 'while no combat *units* . . . [have been] deployed, there was still likely to be plenty of combat *action*'.[35]

One of the key proxies that the West used as a conduit for use of force against ISIS was the Kurdish *Peshmerga* militias.[36] This relationship began soon after the declaration of ISIS's caliphate. Military advisors from the UK, as well as the US and France, were sent to train *Peshmerga* fighters in the use of heavy machine guns, urban warfare operations, and strategic planning. One of the British military advisers noted the increased level of training that this proxy war effort involved compared to other previous indirect interventions: 'One of the things we've agreed to do is not to give them anything without showing them how to use it. That's not always been done in other conflicts.'[37] These *Peshmerga* forces deployed alongside Iraqi Army troops in order to help retake territory around Mosul, Kirku, and Irbil, as well as over the border into Syria, fending off ISIS forces from Kobani. However, in-fighting amongst the different Kurdish factions, namely the PUK, the KDP, and the YPG, made it difficult to homogenise policy towards Kurdish proxies.[38] Yet this did not stop the British government announcing in June 2015 an additional £600,000-worth of military equipment to the *Peshmerga*. This bolstering of the Kurds as proxies came off the back of the deployment of 1,000 UK military trainers, as well as '50 tonnes of non-lethal equipment, heavy machine guns, nearly half a million rounds of ammunition, [and] 1,000 counter-IED VALLON detectors'[39] – as well as a substantial array of weaponry, including machine guns, armoured vehicles, and anti-tank rocket launchers, sent by the German government of Angela Merkel.[40]

The West's initial strong support (politically and logistically) for the Kurdish *Peshmerga* did undermine the 'One Iraq' policy of national unity that had been in place since the regime-changing war that began in 2003. This particular proxy war fostered fears in Baghdad that the West was inadvertently strengthening the case for the break-up of Iraq by catalysing Kurdish independence.[41] In the end, the bigger concern became what to do about weapons given to the Kurds in Syria after President Trump's withdrawal of US forces in 2019 (as discussed in Chapter 2). Senior US commanders urged for Kurdish fighters to be allowed to keep their US-supplied weapons. One Pentagon official was quoted by *Reuters* as saying: 'The idea that we'd be able to recover them is asinine. So we leave them where they are.'[42]

Whilst the Kurds – before being unceremoniously dumped in 2019 – were initially seen as useful proxies in the fight against ISIS inside Iraq and Syria, a disparate coalition of other nationalist fighters were utilised too. But proxy selection was problematic. As Malise Ruthven observed of proxy behaviour in Syria:

> 'Videos of military exploits posted on YouTube became the means by which local militias advertised their services to potential patrons. And while patrons typically used the militias as proxies to advance their interests, the proxies acquired leverage by cultivating multiple patrons, enabling them to exploit their patrons' demand for local influence.'[43]

This created inevitable problems of reliability. One *New York Times* piece in mid-2016 pessimistically concluded that the one-time al-Qaeda-affiliated al-Nusra Front 'has at times shown greater prowess against the Syrian government forces than the CIA's proxies'.[44] Such are the dangers of waging war by proxy.

## The dangers of proxy war-waging against ISIS

The significant level of proxy war activity inside Syria by numerous countries meant that any political solution was going to have to involve those very same nations encouraging their partners inside Syria to come to the negotiating table. But it proved very difficult to break those bonds of alliance between the benefactors and their proxies. Three major consequences of proxy war-waging are worth reflecting on today in light of the fight against ISIS. First is the danger of long-term dependence. On-going financial support will inevitably be needed to rebuild infrastructure inside Syria and Iraq. With the prospect of a large nation-building effort on its hands, all major players inside Syria in particular are going to receive offers of help that could spill over into outright dependence. This is now less of a concern for American proxies given President Trump's surprise withdrawal announcement, but the influx of Russian personnel is a sign that the Kremlin is keen to invest in long-term partnerships in the country.

The second major consequence is the elongation or intensification of the violence. The common view that proxy interventions actually prematurely end an existing conflict is contradicted by evidence that suggests that they actually prolong such conflicts largely because a weak warring faction is boosted to the point of creating stalemate.[45] A flood of weapons or money into an existing war zone gives one or other of the parties involved further motivation and support to fight on, not collapse or seek negotiation. This pattern has repeated itself in the battlespace surrounding the self-declared caliphate of ISIS. In October 2014, Vice-President Joe Biden aired concerns about the overspill effect of the Syrian conflict into the broader Middle East: 'Our allies in the region were our largest problem ... [They] were determined to take down Assad and have a proxy Sunni-Shia war, they poured hundreds of millions of dollars and thousands of tons of weapons into anyone who would fight against Assad'.[46] This, however, fails to reflect the American role in perpetrating exactly the same strategy and compounding the situation further. In 2017, after spending more than $1 billion amid a widespread acceptance at a failure to leverage any significant strategic advantage, the White House ended *Timber Sycamore*, the CIA's three-year long 'train and equip' programme.[47]

Thirdly, it is worth considering how proxy interventions create the conditions for conflict over-spill and 'blowback'. Proxy wars run the severe risk of creating unintended, counter-productive consequences once the war is over. Such blowback can be high profile or subtle in its manifestation. Sometimes the ghosts of proxy wars past do not haunt the corridors of power until decades later. In other words, we are a long way from discovering the true cost of the proxy war being waged against ISIS. A Middle Eastern intelligence official told the veteran foreign correspondent Patrick Cockburn that ISIS fighters 'are always pleased when sophisticated weapons were sent to anti-Assad groups of any kind, because they can always get the arms off them by threats of force or cash payments'.[48] This reality certainly shortens the timeframe in which proxy war benefactors feel blowback from their actions. It took over a decade between the American-assisted mujahedeen ousting of the Soviets from Afghanistan and some of those fighters utilising their experiences to plot the 9/11 attacks and subsequently fight the US military. In Syria the chances of American-sanctioned weaponry being used by ISIS have a much shorter turnaround time. Indeed, the dangers of blowback were realised just months after President Obama approved the 'train and equip' programme in mid-2014. By October that year ISIS uploaded a video to the internet showing a cache of weapons that had been inadvertently dropped from the air over ISIS-held territory. The bundle (one of 27 dropped in that particular airlift) was intended for the Kurdish *Peshmerga* fighters defending the down of Kobane from ISIS fighters.[49] A European Union-funded study in late 2017 concluded that a significant amount of Western-supplied weapons destined for rebel groups in Syria had fallen into the hands of ISIS. These weapons, the study concluded, 'significantly augmented the quantity and quality of weapons available to IS forces – in numbers far beyond those that would have been available through battlefield capture alone'.[50]

But the dangers of proxy war-waging are not just restricted to the absence of a guarantee that all weapons will end up in the hands of your preferred proxy. The reliability of such proxies is also a key issue. This was highlighted in November 2014 when Harakat Hazm and the Syrian Revolutionary Front – two of the main insurgent groups on the receiving end of US arms and money – surrendered to the al-Nusra Front, handing over all their weapons to the al-Qaeda affiliates.[51] The vetting of potential proxies became a significant issue facing the US in particular. One CIA case officer told *Newsweek* that the US was 'completely out of our league' when it came to vetting appropriate 'moderate' rebels inside Syria to fight ISIS. Another operative admitted that 'Syria is a vetting nightmare', concluding that: 'The main problem with plans that arms and train "moderates" – who ominously are moderate only in their fighting abilities – is that it assumes perfect knowledge ... about the people being armed. When in fact there is nothing close to that".[52]

Even the loyalty of purported allies in the war itself is not guaranteed. The Qatari regime has been causing Washington headaches in the fight against ISIS. It is widely acknowledged that the Qataris have been ploughing economic and military aid to the al-Nusra Front. This group, loyal to Ayman al-Zawahiri's al-Qaeda, were Doha's preferred proxy in the battle to depose Assad in Damascus.[53] In October 2014, the Qatari government was forced to deny claims by the US Treasury that elements of the ruling elite were financially supporting ISIS too.[54] The Saudis, on the other hand, initially began pumping money into ISIS as part of a proxy war strategy headed by the then head of Saudi Arabia's intelligence service, Prince Bandar bin Sultan. Western attempts during 2013 to get the Saudis to shift their allegiance to the 'moderate' FSA coincided with Bandar's removal from his post, signalling a shift in the Saudi strategy.[55] Indeed, it was revealed in early 2016 that *Timber Sycamore* – the CIAs train and equip programme to the FSA – had actually become largely bank-rolled by the Saudis, who also provided the bulk of the weapons, leaving the CIA to predominantly lead the training element of the operation. The Saudi General Intelligence Directorate channelled millions of dollars-worth of weapons, including AK-47 assault rifles and TOW anti-tank missiles, to Syrian rebels who were then trained in their use by CIA operatives from a base in Jordan.[56] This represented quite the turnaround in Saudi policy in the conflict.

Some precautions have been taken to minimise 'blowback' from the proxy war being waged against ISIS. Specialist American teams sent to Irbil and Baghdad to deliver weapons to selected proxies were requested to closely log the details of recipients in order to track the whereabouts of the arms in the future.[57] However, there are incidents that give reason for a reflection on the dangers of proxy war-waging. Soon after the deal brokered by the US and Russia in September 2013 that would oversee the decommissioning of Syria's chemical weapons programme, evidence emerged that 'scores of [anti-Assad] Western-backed rebels either quit the field, mutinied, or invited ISIS to raid their Syrian warehouses filled with US-sent aid and supplie'.[58] This blowback was the effect of the strategic confusion at the heart of the West's indirect approach – the US was not anti-Assad enough even for its own proxies. As Michael Weiss and Hassan Hassan have argued: 'given that the rebels' *raison d'etre* was fighting the regime, not ISIS, America's proxy counterinsurgents . . . were bound to cause resentment and disaffection'.[59]

Indeed, the proxy war waged by the West against ISIS has eschewed the veil of plausible deniability with no significant attention being paid to cover up indirect weapons supplies. It may not have been heavily publicised but they were not obfuscated either. This is a key trend in early twenty-first-century proxy warfare – international awareness of their existence is, in itself, a form of power projection. In short, the application of contemporary war by proxy, as epitomised by the fight against ISIS, has become simultaneously more open and less subtle. But this brings with it an additional set of dangers, namely conflict escalation between the intervening global and regional powers (such as when Turkey shot down a Russian jet that had briefly crossed into its airspace in November 2015[60]) and the risks to the reputations of those intervening powers in a legal and ethical context.[61] The proxy war against ISIS, like all modern proxy wars more generally, are the result of an acknowledgment of the management of contending risks. The Western powers who intervened vicariously against ISIS had calculated that the risks of possible escalation, elongation, dependence, and blowback were outweighed by the shorter-term potential for ISIS to be dislodged by local forces, whilst all the while preserving the political and economic capital that would have been expended on a major expeditionary ground war. As one British diplomat, with an air of resigned realism, surmised of the proxy war against ISIS: 'We have entered a post-Sykes-Picot era in which you cannot impose solutions by force. Our foreign policy principles are clear, and the limits of our prosperity and stability are just as clear. We act accordingly'.[62]

## Conclusion

The fight against ISIS has caused significant strategic confusion for the West, especially when deciding which militia groups on the ground inside Syria to adopt as proxies. The case of the al-Nusra Front is typical of this dilemma. Stemming from al-Qaeda, and having formally separated itself from ISIS in the summer of 2014, the al-Nusra Front was at the forefront of insurgent efforts to undermine Bashar al-Assad and take the fight to the Syrian military. Yet, wary of links with members of al-Qaeda's central leadership, the US deliberately targeted al-Nusra Front fighters when air strikes commenced over Syria in September 2014. The result was the al-Nusra Front responded by turning their guns on the 'moderate' groups in the anti-Assad coalition who had been in receipt of support from the US, thus fragmenting the opposition. But, as Jessica Stern and J.M. Berger point out, 'strengthening ISIS would be just one of the possible unintended consequences' of prioritising the removal of Assad.[63] Strategically, for the West, he was the lesser of two evils. Yet one of the biggest strategic miscalculations underpinning the proxy war effort was the false conflation of the just cause of the proxy's fight against Assad and/or ISIS with the appropriateness of a third-party intervention.[64] The short-term focus on attaining tactical victories against ISIS has left the West open to the possibility of longer-term blowback rendered by the strategic disruption to the wider region cause by empowered, well-armed non-state groups that have been used as proxies.[65] The allure of utilising local actors to fight the ground war against ISIS became a quick fix solution to the problem of no appetite for a large-scale invasion. It lacked intrinsic political awareness of the strange combination of militias that were being armed and instead became a technical exercise in weapons dispersal. The lack of conditionality on end-use or return is worrying.

In his bombastic inaugural address in January 2017, President Trump made a direct allusion to what his administration's approach to ISIS would be: 'We will … unite the civilized world against Radical Islamic Terrorism, which we will eradicate completely from the face of the Earth'.[66] Hyperbole aside, initial indications pointed to a new White House line that would be more willing to take direct action against ISIS, through increased SOF activity and more airstrikes (of both a manned and unmanned variety), than pursue a subtler indirect approach that saw weapons and money channelled through proxies. Yet as Chapter 2 highlighted, Trump's unpredictable management of the ISIS campaign has seen him arguably transpose his self-proclaimed 'two simple rules' of domestic policy ('Buy American and Hire American') into his foreign policy agenda, with a greater reluctance to outsource military operations to proxies. The waging of proxy wars relies on a level of trust between benefactor and proxy. President Trump appears to have little trust in many actors on the international stage. To this extent we have seen a departure from the Obama administration's predilection for 'externalising the strategic and operational burden of war to human and technological surrogates'.[67] But with Islamic State undergoing a fundamental post-caliphate organisational reconstruction, the utilisation of proxies as force multipliers to help repel a resurgence of the group may prove too alluring even for Trump.

# 4

# On the Ground and in the Air – Assessing the Special Forces Operations, Local Force Training Missions, and Aerial Campaign Against ISIS

Although there was no large-scale conventional deployment against ISIS, Operation Inherent Resolve did involve operations on the ground and in the air, via incursive Special Operations Forces (SOF) strikes against key targets; 'by, with, and through' local forces; and via a significant aerial bombing campaign against ISIS infrastructure and fighters. An increasing political belief in SOF operations as a panacea to problems caused by violent non-state actors is another post-Iraq War phenomenon. Teams from the US, UK, and France in particular, conducted raids against ISIS leadership figures and launched hostage rescue missions, but significant questions still remain over the strategic effect that small-scale SOF operations can render. Lip service about 'building effective partner forces' emanating from Washington was little more than rhetorical gloss to legitimise the proxy war strategy. The Building Partner Capacity (BPC) programme was a way to safeguard against the need for Western 'boots on the ground' and minimise the political risk of becoming militarily embroiled in another Middle Eastern war. Risk aversion also helps explain the overt reliance on air power as the primary mode of kinetic engagement with ISIS. Exploiting their aerial monopoly, coalition air forces were able to nullify ISIS's initial reliance on conventional force movement and soon forced the group into a fundamental rethink of how they deployed their fighters, but a shadow still hangs over the rate of civilian casualties.

## Special Operations Forces in the war against ISIS

The reliance on SOF throughout the previous wars in Afghanistan and Iraq ensured that covert action was at the heart of US counter-terrorism strategy before the rise of ISIS. Deployment of SOF teams to fight violent non-state actors globally has become a routinised practice since 9/11. High-profile exploits, such as the raid that killed Osama bin Laden, overshadow the more mundane, but ubiquitous, 'advise and assist' missions that has seen US SOF personnel deploy to every continent bar Antarctica.[1] The launch of the 'War on Terror' resulted in the doubling of the size of US Special Operations Command (SOCOM) from 33,000 personnel in 2001 to approximately 70,000 in 2017.[2] Monies for SOF operations under the Obama administration were largely spared the cuts made elsewhere in military spending in the wake of the 2008 global financial crisis. This was to ensure it could keep pace with the ever-increasing requests made for deployments (up from 60 countries in 2009 to an unprecedented 147 by 2015 – that equates to about 70% of all countries on earth).[3]

American Special Operations Forces began arriving at an airhead created at Baghdad International Airport at the end of June 2014. Their official mission was to augment Iraqi self-defence against ISIS through a 'train and assist' mission to national forces. They were joined by British SOF personnel in August, just in time to help coordinate the evacuation of trapped Yazidis on Mount Sinjar, working with combat controllers to call in air strikes on surrounding ISIS forces.[4]

In order to build the capacity of the Iraqi Counter-Terrorism Service, who control special forces in the country, American and other coalition SOF advisors (whose number had been boosted by 130 during the Sinjar crisis by President Obama[5]) first had to improve the training provision of their over-stretched and under-resourced Iraqi counterparts. They overhauled the delivery of the training programme, ultimately adding a greater number of classes, albeit ones of a shorter length than previous iterations as a way of expanding their training but hastening their deployment.[6]

Arguments positing SOF as the silver bullet to America's military dilemma against ISIS were abound as Obama was formulating his strategy against ISIS in September 2014. Retired Major-General Robert H. Scales, former commandant of the US Army War College, used an opinion piece in *The Washington Post* to argue that: 'the only way to defeat the Islamic State … is with a renewed, expanded and overwhelming legion of capable special fighters'. This reliance on SOF, Scales argued, would see a roll out of 'the McChrystal method' that saw Joint Special Operations Command (JSOC) under General Stanley McChrystal take out large numbers of insurgents in Iraq and Afghanistan.[7]

Such arguments seemed to have made an impression on the president. In late 2015, Obama authorised the deployment of an additional 250 SOF into Syria, marking a five-fold increase on the number of US SOF personnel inside that country.[8] They were tasked with training and advising anti-ISIS militia groups, providing extensive symbolism of Obama's willingness to venture US military resources not only in Iraq. This open-ended mission came off the back of previous SOF raids inside Syrian territory, including one in May 2015 by Delta Force commandoes that killed Abu Sayyaf, a senior ISIS commander, and a dozen of his fighters outside Idlib. The Sayyaf raid marked the first time US SOF undertook a mission designed to deliberately kill or capture an ISIS leader not solely to rescue hostages (including the failed attempts to rescue American hostages James Foley in August 2014 and Luke Somers in December 2014).[9] It later transpired that UK Special Air Service (SAS) soldiers wearing American uniforms had provided the initial surveillance mission of Sayyaf's compound and confirmed his presence, effectively green-lighting the Delta Force mission.[10] Another successful Syrian raid reported in the press occurred in the town of al-Kubar in January 2017 that resulted in the death of 25

ISIS members. The target of the raid was thought to be an ISIS-run prison, with the objective of rescuing hostages inside.[11]

It was the targeting of another ISIS prison, this time in the northern Iraqi town of Hawija, back in October 2015 that resulted in the death of a US SOF operative from Delta Force – the first US combat death in Iraq since combat troops had been withdrawn from the country in 2011. A second US SOF fatality, this time a Navy SEAL, occurred in May 2016 as his unit were deployed to assist a Kurdish *Peshmerga* unit under attack from ISIS.[12] But US SOF continued to work closely with Kurdish fighters through coordinating airstrikes and killing or capturing ISIS high-value targets in northern Iraq (via Task Force 27 based in Irbil).[13]

Obama ordered his advisers to start liaising with the Iraqi government about the establishment of a joint special operations task force to tackle the ISIS presence in that country.[14] In the wake of President Trump's surprise withdrawal announcement, Pentagon officials forwarded an option of allowing those US SOF teams based in Iraq to occasionally 'surge' over the border into Syria to undertake specific missions.[15]

Other members of the Global Coalition have utilised their SOF personnel to take on ISIS. Aside from the role the SAS played in the relief of Mount Sinjar and the Abu Sayyaf raid, British SOF have been working alongside Kurdish fighters inside Syria – two of whom were seriously injured in a clash with ISIS forces near the town of Deir al-Zour in January 2019.[16] In addition, the Australians deployed 200 SOF members to Iraq to aid the train and assist mission.[17] However, it has been the French SOF contribution to the war against ISIS that is most noticeable. Since the November 2015 ISIS-inspired terrorist attacks on Paris, the French government had purposely decided to target French ISIS members serving as foreign fighters in Syria and Iraq rather than allow them to return home to possibly perpetrate further atrocities. In May 2017, it was revealed that French special forces had been working with the Iraqi military to 'hunt and kill' French nationals who were in the high echelons of ISIS. Up to 30 French foreign fighters were identified, with SOF teams from France distributing their names and photographs to Iraqi counter-terrorism units.[18] The French SOF teams were not tasked with the kills themselves, instead passing all available intelligence onto their Iraqi colleagues. In part, the SOF presence filled an operational gap created by France's lack of any armed unmanned aerial vehicle (UAV) capability. Yet the outsourcing of these targeted killings provided the French with legal cover from accusations that it directly participated in extra-judicial killing of its own citizens. A French official described this as a 'convenient solution' to tackle the security risk posed by up to 1,700 French foreign fighters in ISIS territory.[19]

'A convenient solution' might indeed be a useful moniker to describe the overall utility to Special Operations Forces to Operation Inherent Resolve. Their provision of surgical kinetic missions that could demonstrate tangible action against high-profile ISIS targets was a soothing salve to national leaders frustrated by a wider campaign that was hamstrung by coalition friction and intractable political differences. But their convenience was undermined by their limited impact. SOF missions provided short-term relief in the face of the need to be seen to be 'doing something' about ISIS, but alone they could not engender any major shift of the strategic pendulum. This is why SOF missions have to be seen in the context of the parallel 'train, advise, and assist' mission to the Iraqi security forces.

## The train, advise, and assist mission

Even though coalition SOF teams had fulfilled regular training missions to 'build partner capacity' inside Iraq from the very earliest days of the coalition action, the 'train, advise, and assist' (TAA) mission on the ground was hampered by political restrictions on the activities of military personnel and by the complex picture of Iraqi national politics. An additional strategic challenge facing this part of the war effort was the influence of Iranian-backed Shia militias, with Tehran's parallel, more aggressive, advise and assist campaign determined to seize contentious territory for themselves (see Chapter 6 for more details of Iran's role in the anti-ISIS fight).[20] The Western TAA mission therefore became essentially about underwriting the short-term future of the Iraqi government from both ISIS and other external powers intent on weakening the state. The complex nature of the Syrian civil war, not least the looming Russian influence over Damascus and their vested interest in seeing Bashar al-Assad remain in power, forced the coalition to adopt an 'Iraq first' approach to the TAA mission against ISIS.[21] The analysis in this section interprets TAA missions as only pertaining to state-based forces. The arming and training of non-state allies is perceived as constituting an act of proxy war given the informal agential relationship between the trainer and the trainee.[22] As such, the actions of the US in regards the multiple anti-ISIS forces inside Syria were analysed in Chapter 3.

The TAA mission essentially meant adopting a 'partnered approach' to war-fighting, the benefits and dilemmas of which were well-enunciated by a 2016 RAND Corporation report, which noted that: '[A]dvisory functions play a critical role in translating capabilities into concrete performance and this ensuring the policy's objective of a lasting defeat of ISIL ... [However] insufficient emphasis on training, advice and assistance can result in a vacuum created by too few troops and police forces to secure cleared areas'.[23] The creation of TAA brigades was the coalition's solution to the problem of having to operate, in military parlance, within a 'manning-restricted, contract-enabled, coalition-force operational environment'.[24] In other words, working with partner forces inside Iraq was the only viable way to take the fight to ISIS when there was no political will to authorise large-scale Western 'boots on the ground'. As such, the TAA mission allowed the coalition to attack ISIS *by, with, and through* the Iraqi security forces.[25]

The US and some other coalition personnel had been providing the Iraqi military with training, advice, and assistance since the 2003 invasion triggered an overhaul in the structure and ethos of the Iraqi security forces. The rise of ISIS provided an opportunity to put this training into practice, but also threw up significant challenges that hampered effectiveness, namely a lack of willing recruits, a lack of armoured vehicles, and force protection concerns.[26] Early reports back from the first wave of US military advisors to Iraqi Army units fighting ISIS in July 2014 indicated that only half of the Iraqi military units they worked with were in an operationally capable state to help retake territory from ISIS.[27]

Another major problem within the coalition was surmounting different interpretations of the scope of the TAA mission. Some key military figures, such as the then US Chairman of the Joint Chiefs of Staff, General Martin Dempsey, advocated a narrow advisory role that was largely technical and tactical in nature. This clashed with a more sustained and strategic assessment of the mission held by commanders in SOCOM who saw this side of the campaign as a long-term effort to influence operations and instil lasting professionalism in indigenous forces.[28] Initial wrangling also took place over whether the pro-government Sunni tribal fighters, almost 20,000 men, would be subject to direct American-led military training.[29] Eventually they were included in TAA exercises.

Early on in the campaign, in September 2014, the Obama administration authorised US troop levels to rise to around 1,400 whose advisory mission was mainly led by SOF soldiers. Specifically they created 12-man teams of SOF personnel who were then assigned to 12 different Iraqi army units at the brigade level or higher. Seven of these US SOF train-and-advise teams were deployed around Baghdad whilst the other five were deployed around the Kurdish city of Irbil. It was initially decided that no US combat advisors would be embedded with Iraqi army units in Anbar province where most of the fighting against ISIS was taking place.[30] The train and assist mission would always take a back seat to force protection.

In November 2014, the White House doubled the number of American combat advisers in Iraq to 3,000. This announcement coincided with the appointment of a new prime minister, Haider al-Abadi, two months earlier. Washington was intent on aligning the priorities of the TAA mission in Iraq with influence over Baghdad's vision for a post-ISIS settlement. The government of Nouri al-Maliki had proved unwilling to arm Sunni tribes, especially in Anbar, who were requesting government assistance to fight ISIS in Iraq's largest province.[31] This doubling of the US TAA effort was contingent upon Congress green-lighting a $1.6 billion 'Iraq Train and Equip Fund' requested by the White House – which itself was only part of a much bigger $5.6 billion budget request for the broader anti-ISIS war effort.[32] This enhanced American TAA mission was designed to train a total of nine Iraqi brigades, totalling 2,500 personnel, as well as three Kurdish *peshmerga* brigades, over a ten-month period with the help of a further 700 trainers from other Global Coalition partner nations.[33]

The retaking of Ramadi by Iraqi security forces in the summer of 2016 was vindication, argued Operation Inherent Resolve commander Lieutenant General Sean McFarland, for 'not fundamentally alter[ing] the paradigm of train and equip, advise and assist'. The coalition held the strategically significant liberation of the city up as a template of successful operational conduct achieved through well-supported indigenous forces against ISIS. McFarland hailed the Ramadi offensive as 'the end of the beginning of the campaign against ISIL'.[34] This experience would prove formative in the battle to retake Mosul later that year.

In total, over the three full years of major combat operations against ISIS (2015–2018) the coalition trained over 130,000 members of the Iraqi security forces and 24,000 police officers in techniques designed to counter the group.[35] The delivery of military 'train the trainer' courses took placed at five locations across Iraq, each led by a different coalition member: Al-Asad, led by Denmark; Besmaya, led by Spain; Dublin and the Kurdistan Training Coordination Center, led by Italy; and Taji, led by Australia.[36]

In February 2018, the US announced it would be expanding its TAA mission by establishing a Coalition Aviation Advisory and Training Team in Iraq to strengthen the aerial warfare capabilities of the Iraqi military.[37] The precarious nature of the long-term US troop presence inside Iraq, caused by questions over President Trump's willingness to commit long term to Iraq's security and to Iraqi anger over the American assassination of Qassem Soleimani (see Chapter 6 for detailed discussion), means that the effectiveness of domestic military forces inside Iraq remain the only viable enduring bulwark against ISIS recidivism. Yet despite this doubling down in the TAA component in the twilight years of Operation Inherent Resolve, some important issues still cast doubts over its utility. The first is the efficacy of the Iraqi Army itself, an organisation with unresolved levels of sectarian infiltration, corruption, and recruitment problems. The second is the way in which the primacy of force protection by remaining coalition units is inhibiting the effective location of TAA missions where they are most needed – in areas with residual groups of ISIS fighters. The deaths of two US service personnel in northern Iraq in March 2020, who were killed whilst conducting train and assist duties with the Iraqi Army, is a testament to the on-going threat posed by pockets of ISIS resistance.[38] The third issue is whether the brigade level at which TAA units are embedded is too high to be effective. Battalion level missions would be more appropriate but would require significantly more resource than Washington currently seems willing to offer. With so many questions hanging over the efficacy of the ground war against ISIS, many Western hopes got pinned on the air war having a greater effect.

## The air war against ISIS

The air war against ISIS started slowly. Strikes came in clusters and lacked sustained coherence. The stop-start nature of the initial campaign was more 'sloth and pause than shock and awe'.[39] Kurdish *Peshmerga* and Iraqi security forces all reported frustration at the limited scope of coalition strikes and the ponderous response to live intelligence on ISIS fighter movements.[40] The staggered entry of nations into the coalition and limited rules of engagement (for example, the UK initially only engaged over Iraq not Syria) was also a source of frustration for both the Americans, who shouldered most of the burden of the air war, and partner forces on the ground.

Only nine of the 74 coalition nations (the US, UK, France, Australia, Jordan, Belgium, Denmark, Canada, and the Netherlands) actually undertook airstrikes against ISIS targets in Iraq and Syria, with the US responsible for half of them.[41] A further four countries – Turkey, Saudi Arabia, Bahrain, and the UAE – conducted operations solely in Syria.[42] After four years of airstrikes, beginning in August 2014, these members of the coalition had conducted 30,008 missions.[43]

Aerial strikes flown by coalition planes fell into two broad categories: deliberate and dynamic. The former were missions chosen in advance against high-value targets, such as key ISIS leaders or oil refineries. The latter were short-notice strikes called in by ground forces engaged with ISIS fighters. Proposed targets were identified by intelligence analysts and passed on to 'targeteers' who used 3D glasses to study computer models of the target site.[44]

Like most other aspects of Operation Inherent Resolve, the air war against ISIS was a predominantly American effort. The US Air Force undertook the vast majority of the airstrikes against ISIS targets that took place from the beginning of Operation Inherent Resolve in 2014 up until President Trump's announcement of a US withdrawal at the end of 2018.[45] The British Royal Air Force (RAF) conducted the second largest amount of air operations, undertaking 1,700 strikes against ISIS targets up to the beginning of 2018. Operating out of RAF Akrotiri in Cyprus, the British contribution involved a mix of combat, transport, as well as intelligence, surveillance, and reconnaissance aircraft, including eight Tornado GR4s (on their last operational deployment before being retired from service in 2019), six Typhoons, two C130s, and Reaper drones.[46]

## The application of air power and drones against ISIS

Before the significant escalation in coalition airstrikes in Syria and Iraq in August/September 2015, ISIS had been relatively free to adopt a conventional operational approach that allowed them to move freely in the absence of a regular air threat. However, after the emphasis on air power by the coalition soared, ISIS was forced to adapt, resorting instead to a habit of urban disguise amid the population. The targeting of flag-laden convoys of ISIS fighters in Humvees forced the group to resort to more conspicuous means of transport.[47] This enforced operational change stalled their 'blitzkrieg' across open territory in Syria and Iraq – and denotes the influence of coalition air power.[48] The lethal effect of coalition airstrikes was significant. In the first year of aerial hits against ISIS targets (August 2014–August 2015), US Central Command (CENTCOM) confirmed that US strikes on 10,600 targets had resulted in the deaths of between 10,000 and 15,000 ISIS fighters.[49]

One of the early priorities of the air campaign was to destroy the large quantity of US-provided heavy equipment, armoured vehicles, and artillery that had been captured off the retreating Iraqi Army during the establishment of the ISIS caliphate. This included M1 Abrams battle tanks and thousands of Humvees. Diminishing the battlefield potency of such requisitioned armaments was undertaken by US Air Force (USAF) sorties of F-22 Raptors and B-1B Lancer bombers using laser-guided Paveway bombs and GPS-guided Joint Direct Attach Munitions (JDAMs). ISIS responded by dispersing concentrations of heavy equipment and concealing it when not engaged in combat.[50]

In autumn 2015, the coalition launched a targeted air campaign based on intelligence seized from the successful raid on the compound of senior ISIS leader Abu Sayyaf, who had been in charge of controlling the caliphate's oil and gas facilities. Airstrikes on the newly discovered location of hundreds of ISIS fuel trucks, as well as oil and gas separation plants, took place with the aim of denting some of ISIS's key income streams.[51] Chapter 5 will go into more detail about the effectiveness of Operation Tidal Wave II on ISIS financing, but suffice to say for now that it marked a key shift in the coalition air war towards more intelligence-driven 'deliberate' strikes and away from 'dynamic' strikes in support of ground forces.

Drones were used in Operation Inherent Resolve to conduct strike missions against ISIS targets, to undertake intelligence, surveillance, and reconnaissance tasks, and to direct other aircraft on their missions. By early 2016, Predator or Reaper drones were responsible for one-third of all US Air Force sorties against ISIS targets – one in five of which involved a missile strike.[52]

Not all drones operated against ISIS were utilised by the air forces of the coalition nations. In September 2015, it was revealed that the CIA's Counterterrorism Center (CTC) had been collaborating with the Joint Special Operations Command (JSOC) to undertake a clandestine drone strike programme, separate from the main drone campaign run by the Air Force. A CIA/JSOC drone strike was thought to be responsible for the death of the British jihadi Junaid Hussain, who had pioneered ISIS's social media strategy.[53] This confluence of the CIA and JSOC in the drone war reunited the two principal units responsible for conducting the search for, and eventual elimination of, Osama bin Laden in 2011.

## Civilian casualties

Air campaigns always run the risk of causing civilian death. Air strikes have proved resistant to efforts to make them an exact science. Operation Inherent Resolve has been no exception to the creation of 'collateral damage' in pursuit of targeting enemy combatants. The coalition claimed responsibility for the deaths of 1,114 civilians in Syria and Iraq during the first four years of air operations.[54] However, this number has been disputed by investigative journalists on the ground and independent think tanks. In 2016, the Airwars project of the Oxford Research Group undertook a monitoring exercise of coalition airstrikes during the first two years of Operation Inherent Resolve. They criticised the coalition for auditing measures of non-combatant fatalities, labelling their casualty assessment process as 'opaque, ad hoc, and significantly biased towards internal military reporting'. Airwars estimated that civilian fatalities were at least ten times higher than what the coalition was reporting (they tallied approximately 1,500 deaths as opposed to the coalition's 152 for that timeframe).[55] A report by two *New York Times* journalists in 2017 went even further by estimating that the civilian death toll was actually 31 times higher than that acknowledged by the coalition.[56] Leading figures in the coalition pushed back against claims of reckless endangerment. Air Chief Marshal Sir Stuart Peach, the UK Chief of Defence Staff, argued in June 2018 that the air component of Operation Inherent Resolve was 'the most carefully planned air campaign in history' whose targeting was 'meticulous'.[57] Indeed, the messaging emanating from the coalition resorted to emphasising the kinetic effect air strikes were having against ISIS cash reserves, oil refineries, and clusters of resistance. The coalition's deputy commander for air, Brigadier General Andrew A. Croft, hailed the air campaign as 'wildly successful' in March 2018.[58] Just don't mention the civilian casualties.

## Evaluating the air campaign

The end of major combat operations against ISIS in late 2017/early 2018 saw a downturn in the need for airstrikes as the group lost large portions of its territory. This prompted many of the countries who had contributed to the air campaign, including Belgium and Australia, to remove their combat aircraft from the region.[59] The air campaign had resulted in some significant victories for the coalition, including the destruction of vast cash reserves, oil production facilities, and the elimination of ISIS commanders on the ground. But this came at a price, both physical (in terms of the civilian casualties incurred) and financial. By the end of 2016, the total cost of the air war against ISIS tipped over the $11 billion mark, averaging out to a daily operational cost of $12.5 million since the first strikes began in August 2014. Of this total figure, the cost of munitions dropped on ISIS targets stood at nearly $2.5 billion.[60] Despite expending huge amounts of money dropping bombs on ISIS, it was the cash reserves of the group that the coalition were simultaneously trying to dry out, as the next chapter will show.

# 5

# Fighting ISIS by Other Means – The Cyber and Finance War

Airstrikes may have provided effective footage to demonstrate kinetic effect against ISIS, and proxies on the ground may have retaken towns and villages street by street as a way of reclaiming territory from them, but there were two key planks of the campaign against ISIS that went largely unseen from public view: the cyber war and the finance war. It is important to understand the effect of these two operational strands, in particular because they reveal elements of tangible success in retarding the functionality of ISIS. ISIS's entire strategic model of maintaining large amounts of territory and administering it like a state proved ultimately too costly to maintain and too vulnerable to manipulation by the coalition. In the face of target airstrikes on cash reserves and oil facilities, ISIS showed a limited economic ability to fund sustained, large-scale military operations that could hold and expand territory given the additional burdens of crippling inflation, restricted access to markets, and limited donations from outside. The financial war against ISIS was therefore one of the more straightforward elements of the campaign for the coalition. By contrast, the cyber war was much slower in producing results in the face of a social media-literate enemy. Restricting the effectiveness of the 'virtual caliphate' was a component of Operation Inherent Resolve that received particular political attention given the need to nullify one of ISIS's key strengths: its online propaganda.

## The cyber war against ISIS

President Obama's off-the-cuff description of ISIS in November 2015 as 'a bunch of killers with good social media' provides not only a potential epitaph for the group but also underlines the vital role played by their cyber capabilities in shaping and disseminating their message.[1] As Colin Clarke has noted, ISIS's online information campaign was effective for three main reasons: first, the group highly valued and rewarded its computer-savvy propagandists; second, the narrative emanating from the group was clear, compelling, and unifying to its supporters; and third, its propaganda themes were obviously focused.[2] For these reasons, the cyber component of Operation Inherent Resolve was imbued with the task of countering ISIS's messaging, nullifying the technical capabilities of ISIS's cyber jihadis, and disrupting the group's operations online. It would be a mission slow to take off, but ultimately an effective one.

### How ISIS used cyberspace

The Al Hayet Media Centre was the control room for ISIS's online activity, producing high-quality material including the 'Mujatweets' series of propaganda videos, its 'One Billion Campaign' on YouTube designed to recruit new volunteers from around the world, podcasts (some recorded in English by British ISIS fighters), and a mobile phone app 'The Dawn of Glad Tidings'.[3] These activities had the aim of communicating their message globally in order to influence, coerce, and recruit.

As ISIS took Mosul in June 2014 and announced the creation of their purported caliphate, the group's social media activities went into overdrive. The Dawn of Glad Tidings app pumped out nearly 40,000 tweets on a single day in the run up to the offensive that took the city.[4] ISIS also coordinated hashtag campaigns amongst its Twitter followers to ensure its messages trended. The group launched its #theFridayofsupportingISIS campaign on 20 June 2014, asking supporters to post pictures of themselves on Twitter publicly waving ISIS flags.[5] One of ISIS's first viral Twitter posts was a set of photos of the capture and execution of Iraqi soldiers posted with threats to other security forces ahead of further offensives towards Baghdad.[6]

The sheer number of ISIS fighters with their own smartphones, shooting videos of their own activities, and uploading them online proved both a blessing and a curse for the group. Simultaneously this massively proliferated the amount of online jihadist material intended to show life on the frontline of the 'caliphate', yet it proved too burdensome for ISIS to control the message or cohere a narrative online.

But ISIS were wary of the potency of certain counter-measures that could be used against them. They therefore tried to limit the exposure of its key leadership figures to cyber-attacks by reducing their level of electronic communication (which could have revealed their location, thus leading to a potential airstrike). ISIS leaders thus resorted to analogue solutions to digital problems: employing couriers to deliver command and control orders in person.[7] It also was forced to adapt even further in response to a belatedly effective coalition cyber strategy by eventually dropping much of its presence on open Western-based platforms like Twitter and instead resorting to encrypted apps like Telegram.[8] ISIS also eventually resigned itself to using the dark web as the critical IT infrastructure of the 'caliphate' became increasingly open to exploitation.[9] In short, ISIS had to sacrifice online visibility for greater online security. In many ways this robbed ISIS of one of its most distinguishing features amongst modern insurgent groups and is now just another 'underground' organisation. Yet for much of its existence as a quasi-state, ISIS's open use of social media rendered counter-intelligence and counter-vulnerability approaches largely redundant for the US and its allies.

Instead, it increased the emphasis on counter-narrative and counter-content initiatives online as well as the launching of an offensive cyber operation by the military.

## Coalition cyber actions against ISIS

Cyber weapons have been utilised against ISIS as a way of both enhancing kinetic effect (through, for example, subverting online command and control [C2] channels to redirect ISIS fighters to areas more favourable for an airstrike) and undertaking acts of organisational disruption (such as by halting money transfers to the group). The American-led cyber effort against ISIS was slow to get going, lacked coordination, and had an uncertain strategic direction. No single agency or branch of the US government initially lay claim to and kept responsibility for shaping the counter-narrative to ISIS's online messaging. Inter-agency cooperation between key players, including the State Department's Center for Strategic Counter-Terrorism Communications and Central Command's (CENTCOM) WebOps team, was reportedly poor.[10]

But a turnaround in cyber effectiveness was initiated by the Obama administration in 2016, with Defense Secretary Ashton Carter bluntly telling US Cyber Command that it needed to 'raise its game against Islamic State'.[11] Electronic surveillance conducted against individual ISIS fighters by the National Security Agency (NSA) was used in conjunction with computer network attacks against the group by US Cyber Command. The aim of this rejuvenated cyber campaign, codenamed Operation Glowing Symphony, was to disrupt ISIS messaging online, prevent further online recruitment, and scramble their C2 procedures.[12] The campaign was coordinated by Joint Task Force 'national mission teams' inside Cyber Command (known as ARES) who 'implanted' an online presence within ISIS networks, learned the online behaviour of certain leaders, and then mimicked their habits to plant deliberately altered information that could be used, for example, to order ISIS units to move positions to areas more vulnerable to US airstrikes.

These Operation Glowing Symphony cyber units also mapped the ISIS cyber network and eventually identified that ISIS was using only ten accounts and servers to coordinate the entire global dissemination of its online material.[13] This realisation allowed ARES operators to hack those accounts and servers, often through rather rudimentary cyber devices like phishing emails to IT administrators within the ISIS network. Once inside the ISIS cyber system they were able to start either disabling it through infesting ISIS servers with malware, or resetting control of pages and servers. Two ARES teams would operate side-by-side – one taking screenshots of ISIS pages for intelligence-gathering purposes, the other actively locking the ISIS cyber propagandists out of their accounts. Once the ten key distribution nodes of the ISIS online machine had been disabled or controlled, Operation Glowing Symphony moved into its next phase, which was to find creative ways to frustrate the cyber presence of ISIS more generally. Described as 'psy-ops with a high-tech twist', this phase of the operation sought to undermine the internet capability of the group by manufacturing slow download speeds on ISIS servers, dropping connections on the computers and phones of ISIS fighters, and installing programme glitches on platforms regularly used by ISIS as a means of constricting their media output and sowing the seeds of discord amongst its web-reliant members.[14] One of the most effective acts was as simple as changing the passwords of ISIS Twitter accounts to deny their propagandists access.[15] Sometimes the old ones are the best. As one Joint Task Force ARES operator put it: 'When you reach through the computer and on the other side is a terrorist organization, and you're that close, and you're touching something that's theirs, that they possess, that they put a lot of time and effort in to to hurt you, that is an incredible rush'.[16] The result was a huge reduction in the ISIS online footprint by late 2017, with the Global Coalition estimating that the group's online propaganda output was 85% less than it was churning out at its peak in August 2015.[17] Many of ISIS's media operations servers were rendered inoperative, with the once influential propaganda magazine *Dabiq* eventually disappearing from the web, the app for its media outlet – the Amaq Agency – ceased to exist, and foreign-language versions of ISIS websites never came back online.[18]

Members of the administration and senior military figures were keen to publicly assert the eventual successes in the cyber domain. Deputy Defense Secretary Robert O. Work boasted of the new strategy: 'We are dropping cyber bombs. We have never done that before.'[19] General Raymond A. Thomas III, head of US Special Operations Command (SOCOM), claimed that cyber weapons were being used alongside traditional military operations to ensure 'the destruction of that adversary [ISIS] on an epic scale.'[20] The open way in which administration officials publicly revealed the successes of cyber efforts against ISIS is unusual given the inherent secrecy regarding clandestine activity. However, the reasons for seeking publicity for the cyber war include demonstrating to the US public that the large amounts of taxpayer money that was invested in the new Cyber Command inside the Pentagon was paying off, as well as signalling to adversaries the American prowess in the cyber domain.[21]

A strange footnote to the cyber war against ISIS involved the hacktivist group Anonymous, who in the wake of the 2015 attack in Paris on the *Charlie Hebdo* magazine office launched their own online battle against the group with the zeitgeisty title '#OpISIS'. Spearheaded by a 25-year-old Boston-based hacktivist, John Chase, the group pieced together a database of 101,000 Twitter accounts linked to ISIS, published it online, and deactivated nearly 150 websites run by or dedicated to the group.[22] This bizarre battle, pitting volunteer hacktivists against cyber jihadists, offers a curious development in the war against ISIS given how it briefly made Anonymous, previously viewed as a mischief-making online nuisance, a de facto ally of the US government in weakening ISIS's online potency. Motivated by a 'strong sense of justice and a disdain for fundamentalists of all stripes', the anti-establishment Anonymous members soon fell into internal disharmony over the implications for web freedom – a key plank of their cause – created by #OpISIS. Although not a coordinated effort, #OpISIS did see hundreds of hacktivists tag Twitter accounts, hack online jihadi forums, and block extremist websites throughout 2015. As one hacker summarised: 'Taking away the free speech from a group that is advocating the end of free speech is delicious fun'.[23]

Although now devoid of a territorial caliphate, ISIS's 'virtual caliphate' does live on, albeit in a much reduced capacity. The group keeps finding new ways to disseminate messages and distribute cyber propaganda. Even after the fall of Raqqa in October 2017, ISIS social media channels were still pumping out messages emphasising latent power and endurance.[24]

## The finance war against ISIS

Stemming the flow of ISIS funding was one of the coalition's five 'lines of effort' against the group, placing counter-financing at the heart of the West's strategy. Cutting off the money flow to an enemy combatant is an important marker of campaign success as it destabilises the environment in which they could effectively foot the bill to maintain current operations or plan future ones.[25] As such, the Counter ISIS Finance Group (CIFG) was established in January 2015 as one of the five working groups created by the coalition to manage key strategic planks of its war effort.[26] By the end of that same year the US Treasury estimated that ISIS had generated revenue within its territory totalling nearly $1 billion, half of which was made up by oil sales and around a third from internal taxation on the population.[27] This made ISIS the richest terrorist group the world had ever seen. However, if we understand their territorial control and governance structures as actually constituting a quasi-state needed to maintain infrastructure and provide public amenities, then the Islamic State would rank as one of the poorest states in the world.[28] Such a perception would become important to understanding how those financial resources became rapidly depleted because the sustainability of ISIS's economic model was inextricably linked to the sustainability of its territorial 'caliphate' given the need to finance military operations that would hold or expand areas under their control.

### How ISIS was financed

The main sources of ISIS funding were: taxes collected in controlled areas; resource smuggling, especially oil; hostage ransom payments; looting of historical sites for antiquities; and foreign donations.[29] Captured battlefield documents and media reports on the ground have revealed much about the ISIS system of financing, including a desire to learn lessons from the financial conduct of their predecessor group Al-Qaeda in Iraq (AQI), especially the distribution of money to local cells and an early reliance on funds brought in by foreign fighters.[30] The group was certainly keen to set up a viable financial system in order to provide basic public services. Indeed, the first ever issue of *Dabiq*, ISIS's English language magazine, noted the group's purported intention to 'pump millions of dollars into services that are important to Muslims.'[31]

ISIS imposed a loose tax regime on areas under its control in order to sustain its proto-state and military ambitions. This included a customs tax on goods passing through its territory (the fee was set locally); a business tax payable by shopkeepers and bigger companies to be allowed to trade (again, the rates varied across the territory); a utilities tax that was levied on business owners for use of electricity and water drawn from resources under ISIS control; and a religious tax (or *jizyah*) on Christians who did not convert to Islam (the alternative to payment was death).[32]

The 2015 migration crisis (created in part by the rise of ISIS) was a major financial boon for the group. They used their control of major border crossing points between Syria and Turkey to tax people traffickers for each migrant who had in turn paid them to cross through the caliphate on their way to Europe. At the height of the migration crisis in the summer of 2015, ISIS was generating $500,000 per day from taxes paid by people traffickers, exceeding the income from tax on illicit oil supplies.[33] Oil provided a short-lived boon to its financial status. Most oil extracted from reserves in ISIS territory was used internally in vehicles or for heating systems, not for export. A lack of technical personnel and limited access to wider markets restricted the group's capacity to reap large economic dividends in the long run from oil. It should also be noted that ISIS were also at the whim of the global financial markets, in as much as their oil-smuggling profits were severely hit by a reduction in the crude oil price in 2014–2015.[34] Free market capitalism proved an unwitting yet effective counter-terrorist finance tool.

Economic efficiency inside the caliphate was also hampered by strict rules limiting female participation in the labour force and a failure to recruit enough professionals to keep key sectors functioning. Popular support for ISIS in Mosul in 2015 became strained as news spread that the group was not spending the 2.5% charitable tax (or *zahat*) on all income towards good causes as promised and had been channelling the money to buy weapons instead.[35] Simply, the conditions conducive to economic growth, including an educated and healthy workforce, access to credit and insurance markets, and legally protected investments were absent in ISIS-controlled areas.[36] The estimated decline in total ISIS revenue from $1 billion in 2015 to just under half that a year later suggested a rapidly shrinking economy that was hampered by large population decline and a poorly managed tax collection system.[37] Coalition military action targeting oil wells, cash depots, and the wider infrastructure of the caliphate further shrank ISIS's revenue, territory, and tax base.

## Coalition military action against financial targets

It is a strange irony that one of the most effective coalition measures taken against the financial standing of ISIS involved not subtle manipulation of the international finance system or targeted sanctions against key donors, but blunt kinetic force. Airstrikes against ISIS-controlled oil and gas facilities were codenamed Operation Tidal Wave II – a contemporary nod to the initial Operation Tidal Wave in the Second World War that saw Allied aircraft bomb Nazi-controlled oil refineries in Romania. In November 2015 alone, coalition airstrikes destroyed 399 fuel trucks containing oil from ISIS refineries heading for sale on the black market. This was in addition to strikes that destroyed three whole refineries near the Syrian border with Turkey.[38] In the 15 months up to the end of 2016, coalition airstrikes destroyed over 1,200 fuel trucks in total.[39] A report by the inter-governmental Financial Action Task Force (FATF), which coordinates global responses to money laundering and terrorist financing, concluded that coalition airstrikes had played a large role in diminishing ISIS's ability to extract, refine, and sell petroleum products, thus significantly reducing a key revenue stream.[40]

Yet it was not just oil that was a prime target for coalition airstrikes. Large cash storage depots were also hit. The US Treasury estimated that airstrikes on these facilities in 2015 'incinerated at least tens of millions and possibly more than a hundred million dollars' in cash reserves, severely damaging the group's liquidity.[41] The resultant financial pressures on the group played a role in ISIS suspending the payment of death benefits to the families of deceased fighters.[42]

Salaries paid to ISIS fighters dropped by up to 50% in the wake of these strikes, inevitably impacting recruitment and retention rates.[43] As one NBC News story bluntly put it, the coalition counter-financing strategy could be summed up as: 'follow the money, then blow it up'.[44] Airstrikes proved hugely effective in crippling the financial reserves of ISIS and destroying large quantities of a key revenue stream. Yet there were non-kinetic means that leveraged the international financial system against ISIS too.

## Using the international finance system against ISIS

In October 2016, Acting Under Secretary of the US Treasury Adam Szubin outlined a two-pronged approach to countering ISIS finances using the international finance system. One line of action was nominally defensive, involving enhancing the transparency of the finance system in order to disrupt money flows to and from the group. The second line of action was more offensive in as much as it sought to impose targeted sanctions on known ISIS financiers.[45] This would involve combing through an enormous amount of financial intelligence (FININT) to trace transactions and monitor money laundering efforts. In 2015, the Financial Crimes Enforcement Network (FinCEN) inside the US Treasury was receiving around 55,000 daily reports from financial institutions around the world that it would screen for ISIS's financial fingerprints. This included checking monetary transactions involving any known ISIS affiliates, IP addresses, email addresses, or phone numbers.[46] Such procedures were symptomatic of the way in which the 9/11 attacks had spurred a significant shift in state policies regarding tackling terrorist finances away from cracking down on proceeds from drug-smuggling and towards anti-money laundering initiatives.[47]

Pressure was put on member states of the United Nations by Secretary General Ban Ki-moon in early 2016 to resort to a range of methods to counter the finances of ISIS. This included adhering to a sanctions regime in regards to known ISIS affiliates and working more closely with the private sector (especially in banking, antiquities, and internet service providers) in order to close down ISIS's channels of lucrative criminal enterprise.[48] The sanctions regime proved only moderately effective. The assets of some donors and foreign fighters were frozen, but only two prosecutions for financing ISIS have been secured – one in the US and one in the UK.[49] Yet what is significant was the absence of major foreign donors to ISIS. The group lacked the personal wealth of an Osama bin Laden-type figure to bankroll operations, although in October 2014 the US Under Secretary of the Treasury for Terrorism and Financial Intelligence, David Cohen, did describe Kuwait and Qatar as being 'permissive jurisdictions' for terrorist financing, including that of ISIS.[50]

The entire banking system in Iraq was made vulnerable by the ISIS presence in large parts of the country. The Iraqi authorities estimated that ISIS had looted a total of $223 million from banks in Iraqi territory under the group's control.[51] In order to shore-up the country's banks, the US Treasury in conjunction with the Central Bank of Iraq (CBI) isolated 90 banks within ISIS-controlled territory from the international and Iraqi banking systems to shut down potential money transfers that could aid the group. In addition, one hundred currency exchange houses were blacklisted by the CBI from participation in dollar auctions because of suspected ISIS links.[52] These measures ensured that ISIS had to maintain its usage of vaults and depots as cash storage facilities that proved incredibly vulnerable to coalition airstrikes. The US also set up a separate Bilateral Commission to Counter Terrorist Financing with the Iraqi government to more closely monitor ISIS money flows in and out of the country.[53]

Counter-financing planning was also undertaken at the highest levels of the US intelligence community. In 2016, the US Office of the Director of National Intelligence commissioned a report that role-played three possible futures for ISIS and their implications on financing. One scenario was based on ISIS affiliates globally plundering their local economies; one in which ISIS continued to expand its state-like control to leverage finance from the population; and one in which a rapid expansion and attainment of pan-regional dominance allowed them to utilise a much wider financial structure.[54] Clearly this was 'worst case scenario' planning, given that the latter two scenarios implicitly relied on a failure of coalition strategy, yet it gives an insight into the awareness of the intrinsic relationship between ISIS's financial health and its territorial viability.

## Assessing the financial war against ISIS

Military action proved more effective at reducing ISIS's financial resources than orthodox counter-financing initiatives involving asset freezing. This is in part due to the way in which illicit terrorist finances are often well hidden from traditional banking structures. But the coalition did not produce a successful non-kinetic answer to the problem of ISIS financing. Operation Tidal Wave II essentially turned financial records into intelligence that decided targets for airstrikes. Kurt Gredzinski, the Counter-Threat Finance Team Chief at US Special Operations Command (SOCOM), admitted that it was 'the first time in my recollection that we strategically targeted based on threat finance information'.[55] FININT played a big part in facilitating kinetic effect against ISIS. As one senior intelligence official told NBC News in 2016: 'Money is often a more effective way to track and target than eyeballs or hearing'.[56]

Over a year after the fall of the caliphate, US intelligence officials still estimated ISIS to be sat on around $400 million in stolen cash and looted gold, paving a financial path to viable future operations. Much of this money was laundered throughout the Middle East in the

months after the fall of Raqqa in 2017.[57] These large illicit reserves
that are available to the remnants of the group are reason alone not to
underestimate the capacity of ISIS to pose a future threat, not just to
rural areas within proximity of their pockets of resistance but also to
the national security landscape of Iraq, Syria, and the wider region –
not to mention the possibility of future attacks against the West.[58]

# 6

# The Alternative War: Russia, Iran, and Turkey Against ISIS

The war against ISIS was not an exclusively Western one, or one that only drew Sunni nations in, despite the assumptions that could be drawn from the membership of the Global Coalition. An alternative set of uncoordinated yet collectively significant interventions by Russia, Iran, and Turkey fundamentally shaped the strategic landscape in which Operation Inherent Resolve was trying to operate. Ironically, tackling ISIS was not the major motivating factor behind these parallel campaigns, yet the space in and around the ISIS caliphate witnessed three non-coalition nations wage more strategically driven and risk-taking campaigns than the American-led multi-national effort could ever muster. The coalition was outplayed by its rival regional powers.

Russia's priority during its intervention was not defeating ISIS but keeping its ally Bashar al-Assad in power. Moscow steadily escalated its military presence in Syria, moving from its initial role of advising the Syrian military and conducting airstrikes to an outright combatant role via the deployment of soldiers and military police to help secure strategically important areas such as Aleppo in 2017 and the Damascus suburb of Eastern Ghouta in 2018. Russia also had a hand in reshaping the structure of the Syrian Army, including overseeing the creation of two new corps.[1] Helping the Syrian military neutralise militia groups that simultaneously were opposed to both Assad and ISIS put the Russian strategy directly at odds with the explicit political objectives of the coalition. Yet President Putin pursued his interests regardless and came away with more strategic victories than can be claimed by any other intervening power.

Beyond assassinating the key Iranian figurehead, the US has had no answer to Tehran's increasing power base in the wider region. Qassem Soleimani proved integral to Iran's implementation of a grander strategic plan, in the making long before they took advantage of the regional chaos caused by the rise of ISIS, to become a strong counter-weight to Saudi Arabia in the Middle East and perpetual thorn in the American side. Iran's ability to build a network of Shia forces westwards from Tehran to the Mediterranean Sea has created a 'land bridge' of influence. Tehran's explicitly sectarian intervention has reinforced their power of direction over the Shia-dominated politics of Iraq, much to Washington's exasperation.

Finally, this chapter considers the Janus-faced intervention of Turkey. Although a Global Coalition member, the lip service paid by the government of Recep Tayyip Erdoğan to the need to defeat ISIS was exposed by Ankara's predominant emphasis on exploiting the security situation to massively expand their military action against their long-standing Kurdish enemies. Turkey was a strategically vital nation in the war against ISIS, but not in the ways always necessarily conducive to meeting the goals of Operation Inherent Resolve.

## Russia's war in Syria: more pro-Assad than anti-ISIS

Moscow's war in Syria was its biggest and arguably most significant operation outside its traditional Soviet-era sphere of influence since the USSR collapsed.[2] Their increasingly powerful role in the politics of the current Syria crisis was years in the making. It was a confluence of national, regional, and international dynamics that led President Vladimir Putin to enhance Russian influence with his ally Bashar al-Assad, gain a greater strategic foothold in the Middle East, and posit

Russia as a bulwark to perceived Western aggression. Much of this greater Russian activity inside Syria took the form of an indirect supply of weapons, a large air campaign, and the deployment of military personnel. Moscow, in short, waged an effective war inside Syria that strategically outmanoeuvred the West by shifting the emphasis onto the maintenance of Assad's rule rather than the defeat of ISIS.

Russian efforts to warn against Western military strikes in response to the chemical gas attack on the Damascus suburb of Douma on 9 April 2018 elevated Moscow's position as outright guardian of Assad's regime. This marked a continuation of Russia's intervention in his favour that had been building for some time. It is no coincidence that Russia attempted to seize the initiative in Syria soon after the Americans spectacularly cancelled their 'train and equip' programme for their favoured rebel groups inside the country. With Washington's proxy war effort in Syria faltering, Moscow shifted gear. But Vladimir Putin's priorities were less about tackling ISIS in Syria, and more about ensuring that his ally Bashar al-Assad remained in power in Damascus. Putin has been playing the long game.[3]

In July 2015, the crash of two Russian-made drones in rebel-held Syrian territory flagged up the levels of support (and sophistication of equipment) being supplied by Moscow to Damascus. This event seemed to have encouraged the Russians to drop any pretence of their presence in Syria. Russian military and intelligence advisers began to move openly around the country. The docking in late August that year in Latakia of the RFS *Nikolay Filchenkov* and the unloading of its contents (trucks, armoured personnel carriers, and more military advisers) marked the beginning of a 'sustained sealift' that ratcheted up levels of indirect assistance on offer from President Putin. This was soon complemented later the same month by a massive airlift sustained by Antonov cargo planes that deposited a large amount of military supplies, such as air defence systems, at the Basel al-Assad airbase in Jadleh. These were accompanied by 48 Russian Air Force strike aircraft who were to provide the mainstay of Russia's parallel direct intervention against ISIS and, more controversially, anti-Assad rebel targets.[4] This significant escalation wrong-footed the West given that their own preferred proxies were now being undermined by Moscow. As one *New York Times* piece observed: 'For the first time since Afghanistan in the 1980s, the Russian military ... has been in direct combat with rebel forces trained and supplied by the CIA'.[5]

The contending proxy wars created a stark contradiction. As David Kilcullen has noted: 'whereas [the Americans] were intervening *against* ISIS, the Russians were intervening *in support* of Assad'.[6] The US and Russia have adopted the same means, but different ends in Syria. It understandably created friction between Washington and Moscow, even if publicly President Obama denied it, arguing in August 2016 that: 'We're not going to make Syria into a proxy war between the United States and Russia ... This is not some superpower chessboard contest'.[7] Whether that was the intention or not, it is precisely what happened – thus highlighting the significant, and often unintended, dangers associated with the waging of proxy war, as Chapter 3 highlighted. A single offensive by anti-Assad rebels against the Syrian Army in the second week of October 2015 encapsulated the de facto proxy war taking place between the US and Russia. Groups affiliated with the Free Syria Army, such as Tajamu al-Izza, used US-supplied BGM-71 TOW (tube-launched, optically-tracked, wire-guided) anti-tank missiles that they nicknamed 'Assad tamers' to destroy what it claimed were up to 24 Russian-made tanks of regime forces on the first day of the offensive alone[8] – a sign of the inadvertent proxy war developing between the two former Cold War foes.

Yet the Russians were also keen to engage kinetically themselves, not just indirectly through proxies. A key way this was achieved was through the utilisation of air power. A month after the establishment of the caliphate Moscow offered the government in Baghdad an emergency shipment of Su-25 jets for use by the Iraqi Air Force against ISIS targets.[9] Just over a year later, in September 2015, the Kremlin began a massive aerial bombing campaign. Russian jets flew over 6,000 sorties in a four-month period. They began with about 60 daily sorties being undertaken but this soon tailed off as target selection became more limited. Yet the bombing of a Russian civilian airliner by jihadists in Egypt and the crisis caused by the downing of a Russian Su-24 jet in Turkish airspace in November 2015 saw the Kremlin ramp up the pace of air operations to over 120 sorties per day.

Questions remain, however, over whether they were hitting ISIS targets, as they claimed. Russian aircraft were spotted dropping bombs during this period on civilian areas held by anti-Assad rebel groups, which coincided with a large ground offensive by Assad's allies including Iran and Hezbollah.[10] A major report from the Washington-based think tank the Center for Strategic and International Studies described this as the 'punishment phase' of the Russian strategy, designed to erode civilian will to support the rebels.[11] The US government openly accused Russia of 'throwing gasoline on the fire' by targeting the groups fighting Assad.[12] It soon became clear that the transfer of the Khmeimim airbase from the Syrian to the Russian Air Force at the start of the Russian air campaign (not to mention the 28 aircraft and 2,000 military personnel that arrived there afterwards) was not to bolster the anti-ISIS campaign but bolster the pro-Assad one instead. But within two weeks of the first Russian strikes against the anti-Assad militants reports of significant ISIS gains in that area of northwest Syria began to emerge. By the second week of October 2015, ISIS had taken six villages around Aleppo, close to an important rebel supply route to Turkey.[13]

The coordination of Russian air strikes and Syrian/Iranian/Hezbollah ground offensives became a clear pattern as the conflict rumbled on. ISIS was not the main target – it was the array of anti-Assad rebel groups. Indeed, there were many leading political and

military figures in Moscow, including Chief of the General Staff
Valery Gerasimov, who wondered aloud whether ISIS was actually a
construct of the United States who were using Operation Inherent
Resolve as a Trojan Horse to reorder the wider region.[14]

Russia has not confined itself to intervention only in Syria.
Alongside the proliferation of its military assistance programme in
support of Assad, a small but ultimately influential intelligence liaison
team was deployed to Baghdad to create a joint Russian-Iranian-
Iraqi-Syrian operations room. Led by a three-star Russian general,
this unit coordinated intelligence sharing in the fight against ISIS.
This was not only an effort to undermine, or even replace, US-led
efforts to apply a joint direct-indirect strategic approach to the war
against ISIS, but also marked a leap in Russian expeditionary action
outside its traditional post-Soviet 'sphere of influence'.

The war against ISIS on Syrian soil has been a domestic counter-
terrorism success for the Kremlin. President Putin clearly feared that
the rise of ISIS would inspire Islamists inside Russia and went about
trying to mitigate the internal threat posed by the group.[15] There are
some non-corroborated reports that Moscow actively encouraged
Russian jihadis to travel to Syria and may even have assisted them in
attaining passports to get there. The purported logic of the Federal
Security Service (FSB) in allowing this was to clear Russia of its most
potent internal terrorist threats, namely radicals from the North
Caucus areas of Chechnya and Dagestan. Some Russian press reports
quoted FSB sources as estimating that up to 5,000 Russian nationals
had joined ISIS by 2014 and they only expected 300–400 to ever
return. As a RUSI report put it, 'the potential tenfold reduction in the
number of violent extremists within Russia could be the most radical
achievement of the country's counter-extremist policy ever'.[16]

As Bettina Renz has pointed out, the Russian intervention in Syria
has symbolised a 'remarkable military revival' for Moscow after the
humiliation of the first Chechen War and the underwhelming outcome

of the conflict with Georgia in the previous decade.[17] Putin's Syrian adventure had, unlike those recent interventions, resulted in few losses, allowed Russia to showcase new military technology (including cutting-edge precision-guided cruise missiles) and, crucially, demonstrated extensive sea and air-lift capabilities needed to wage a military campaign beyond the boundaries of the former Soviet states. Compounded by the annexation of Crimea in 2014, the Syrian operations have proved worrisome for the West given the additional foothold in southern Europe and the wider Middle East through the building of a naval base in the Syrian warm water port of Tartus that now offers Russia a permanent presence on NATOs southern flank in the Mediterranean.[18] Collectively, this paints a stark picture of a Russian political and military renaissance.

Russia may have had fewer troops in the region during the conflict than the entirety of the Global Coalition and may have lacked other regional partnerships beyond the bonds with Bashar al-Assad's regime and a clutch of proxies (including Hezbollah and some influential Russian private military companies, in particular the Wagner Group[19]), but in terms of engineering a preferred outcome Russia has had a much better war than the US and its allies. Russia was bolder in its intervention. Unlike the West, they put boots on the ground. In August 2018, the Russian Defence Ministry confirmed that in nearly three years of military operations a total of 63,000 troops (including 434 generals) had deployed to Syria. In addition, it claimed that 90% of all Russian Air Force combat pilots had flown sorties over the country.[20] This level of deployment constituted a big risk for Vladimir Putin, but he was driven by a desire to augment Russian interests in a pliant, yet strategically useful state, whilst simultaneously frustrating US regional designs, in order to attain cost-effective military objectives.[21]

Crucially, Putin made the conflict about the longevity of Assad's rule not about the destruction of ISIS. It was therefore strategically more committed and operationally more focused than a multi-national coalition effort to roll up an insurgent group through assistance to partner forces and from air strikes. Perversely, the main Russian contribution to the anti-ISIS campaign was to facilitate the Syrian regime's forces to claw back its own territory. The Kremlin's strategy was simple: maintain Assad to defeat ISIS. Unwittingly the West had to come to accept the cruel reality of that strategy too.

## Iran's war: Soleimani and the 'road to the sea'

Since the days of Mahmoud Ahmadinejad in power, Iranian foreign policymaking has been the preserve of the Islamic Revolutionary Guards Corps (IRGC). This vanguard of the ideology of the revolution has long secured its place at the heart of Iranian political life. The IRGC and Major-General Qasem Soleimani, the ubiquitous commander of its irregular warfare unit the Quds Force, and not necessarily President Hassan Rouhani, proved to be the driving force behind Iranian action in Syria and Iraq against ISIS.[22] Soleimani was the public face of Iranian action after stepping out of the shadows to accept plaudits for turning the battle on the ground in Iran's favour. His assassination by the US in January 2020 symbolised his embodiment of Iran's effective, and ruthless, pursuit of greater regional dominance – and marked the lowest, and most dangerous, point of US-Iranian relations since the 1979 revolution. Inside Iraq Soleimani and the Revolutionary Guard helped enhance the capacity of a number of proxy groups that had a close relationship with the national military, including al-Nujaba, Asa'ib Ahl al-Haq, the Badr Organisation, and Kata'ib Hezbollah.[23] Inside Syria the IRGCs primary creation was the National Defence Force (NDF), a Shia volunteer militia group designed to defend positions from ISIS incursion.[24]

Iranian strategy during the war against ISIS operated at three different levels: try and defeat Sunni radicalism and terrorism on its national borders; get the upper hand over the Saudis for regional dominance; and make a global statement by undermining US interests.[25] To a significant extent Tehran has successfully fulfilled its objectives. It has provided unabashed assistance to its allies through a targeted military deployment in the face of Western reticence to put boots on the ground. Unlike the West, Iran's policy has not largely been about the short-term selection of proxies. It is based on a more developed grand strategy designed to achieve the total security of the regime through the cultivation of a wider set of regional relationships, facilitated by the Revolutionary Guard, whilst avoiding a major confrontation. They have been adept soft power wielders in Shia countries too.[26]

The shaping of this strategy was the result of some initial miscalculations. Like most other states globally, Iran was caught off-guard by the rapid rise of ISIS. An initial policy of downplaying the threat posed by the group soon switched to a more proactive one, driven by the alarm at the possibility of infiltration into Iranian territory.[27] After the fall of Mosul to ISIS is June 2014, Tehran initiated daily deliveries of 140 tonnes of military equipment to Baghdad, including rocket launchers and machine guns. In July 2014, the Iranian's returned Iraqi Air Force SU-25s that had been captured during the 1980–1988 Iran-Iraq War in order to bolster Baghdad's military capabilities.[28] When ISIS captured the Kurdish town of Jalawla, just 20 miles from the Iranian border, Tehran reportedly ordered M60 tanks and army units to support the *Peshmerga* counter-offensive to retake the town. Additional Iranian military assistance helped Kurdish forces retake other towns from ISIS in late 2014, including Amerli and Suleiman Beg.[29] Analysis of the usually restrictive Iranian media in late 2015 revealed that 67 Iranians had been killed fighting in Syria during October and November of that year alone, including a high-ranking Revolutionary Guards general whose funeral eulogy was delivered by Ayatollah Khamenei himself.[30] This increasing openness about casualties can be seen as part of a desire by Tehran to be seen as a major player in the conflict and thus the wider region after the Russian-led campaign against Syrian rebels intensified in September 2015, as discussed earlier in this chapter.

Another major factor weighing on Tehran's decision-making calculus was a fear of the territorial disintegration of Iraq after ISIS. A unified, majority Shia Iraq would be easier to dominate than three separate Sunni, Shia, and Kurdish states, as had been mooted multiple times since the US invasion in 2003. This motivation directly informed Tehran's proxy war strategy. Indeed, Iran was one of the first nations to send weaponry to Kurdish groups in northern Iraq.[31] From that moment on Iran adeptly leveraged influence by playing different Kurdish factions off against other regional powers. Iranian connections with the PKK made Turkey wary of Tehran's influence; likewise Tehran's links to the Syrian off-shoot of the PKK, the PYD, and its paramilitary YPG forces, established a greater foothold over events in Syria; all whilst the Iraq-based PKK were utilised to off-set the influence of less pliable Kurdish groups in Iraqi politics, namely the KDP.[32] In areas under PKK control, by late 2014 the Iranian's coalesced all *Peshmerga* units, PKK and YPG fighters, as well as other Shia paramilitaries, under a unified command structure led by the Revolutionary Guard. The Iranians used this to pool intelligence, weapons, and other logistics with their proxies. One Kurdish fighter told the International Crisis Group of the extent of the Iranian support: 'Iranian military support is for all Iraqi forces, including *peshmergas*, and this is crucial for the fight against Daesh ... There were Iranian technical teams to train our forces on some advanced weapons, and Iranian artillery units joined in the fighting.'[33]

The sectarian religious tensions at play in Syria and Iraq have created the conditions for an escalating regional proxy war between Shia Iran and rival Sunni powers. Evidence emerged in 2013 that the Quds Force and Lebanese Hezbollah had been training the National Defence Force

(NDF), a pro-Assad paramilitary unit it had helped create. With tens of thousands of recruits, each brigade of the NDF was nominally led by a Revolutionary Guard commander whose job was as much ideological as it was operational.[34] General Soleimani helped the Badr Organisation, the leading Shia militia group in Iraq, retake Jurf as-Sakhr, a town south of Baghdad, from ISIS in October 2014.[35] This success came to crystallise the importance of indirect support to Iraqi militias in the anti-ISIS fight given the inability of the Iraqi state to achieve victories itself. After Iraqi prime minister, and leading Shia figurehead, Nouri al-Maliki left office in 2014, he became an instrumental figure in Hashd Al-Shaabi (Popular Mobilization Forces, PMF), which was an umbrella organisation of predominantly Shia militia groups. Nominally run under the auspices of the Iraqi interior ministry but sponsored by the Quds Force and dominated by the Badr Organisation, the PMF operated in a structure parallel to the Iraqi national army in an effort to coordinate the fight against ISIS.[36]

Similar levels of Shia militia influence were visible in Syria too. In the summer of 2015, Bashar al-Assad opted to enlist the help of a coterie of proxies, including Hezbollah fighters and Iranian 'volunteers' from the Revolutionary Guard, in order to push ISIS out of the strategically important parts of southern Syria.[37] Pro-Assad militia forces sponsored by the Iranians also proved instrumental in fighting with regime forces around Aleppo in 2016.[38] The use of such proxies appeared to be strategic as well as operational. There was a widespread understanding that Iran had been using Shia militias as proxies to secure a land corridor stretching west from the Iran-Iraq border across into northern Syria to the Mediterranean, vastly expanding Tehran's influence in the Arab world. Spearheaded by Qasam Soleimani, this 'road to the sea' would see Shia villages, towns, and cities linked by roads protected by loyal Shia militias as a means of solidifying regional hegemony[39] – the exact reason why Soleimani became such a target for the US.

Since the 1990s, Soleimani had been successfully building a network of Shia proxies around the region in an effort to enhance the Iranian sphere of influence. A key figure in facilitating the Shia resistance in Iraq against the American invasion after 2003, he moulded the Quds Force into a preeminent exponent of asymmetric warfare. He had also opportunistically turned the rise of ISIS and the wider regional instability it wrought to Iran's advantage by taking a high-profile role in directing Shia paramilitary resistance to the group whilst simultaneously undermining the Western powers also fighting ISIS.[40] His assassination by the Americans is a strange, tangential coda to Western military operations against ISIS. The Iranian threats of retaliation against US bases inside Iraq sparked the Global Coalition to announce it was suspending its anti-ISIS operations to focus on force protection of service personnel.[41] Against the backdrop of the Iraqi parliament passing a non-binding resolution calling for the withdrawal of all American troops from their soil in the wake of the Soleimani killing,[42] the US military command in Baghdad erroneously released a draft statement that seemed to confirm that the US was pulling all its forces out of the country, before the Pentagon clarified its position.[43]

Increased Iranian influence in the region is a lasting legacy of the failure of the West's war and a testimony to Soleimani's important facilitating role. The oscillation of the American position over Iran's interference in Syria is partly to blame. In October 2014, President Obama wrote the Iranian Supreme Leader, Ayatollah Ali Khamenei, a letter that 'raised the possibility of US-Iranian cooperation in fighting Islamic State if a nuclear deal is secured'.[44] Although a nuclear deal with Iran was eventually agreed in April 2015, it is clear that no cooperation between Washington and Tehran in the fight against ISIS was ever forthcoming. Yet it remains significant that the defeat of ISIS – a mutual goal – was used as potential leverage in high-level nuclear diplomacy. This would all end with the arrival of the Trump administration. Not only did the new president withdraw from the Joint Comprehensive

Plan in May 2018 but his removal of US personnel from the region left a vacuum of influence that the Iranians could fill. In the wake of Trump's withdrawal announcement, US Secretary of State Mike Pompeo dialled up the pressure on Iran to end its proxy involvement in the country, promising to 'expel every last Iranian boot' from Syria and threatened to withdraw US aid money from the Syrian government until Iranian personnel had departed.[45] He did not make clear how this would be enforced by the imminently departing US. Clearly Iranian involvement was still irksome for the White House but not so significant that it necessitated staying. The asymmetry of interests between Washington and Tehran on display over the future of Syria and the shape of the wider Middle East is stark.

## Turkey's complicated war

The Turkish government of Recep Tayyip Erdoğan never went out of its way to offer leadership in the war against ISIS because the chance to use ISIS as a useful stooge to eliminate a common enemy – Kurdish fighters – was too tempting an opportunity for Ankara to miss. The Kurdish issue, for so long a thorn in the side of successive Turkish governments since the outbreak of the Kurdish Workers' Party (PKK) insurgency in 1984, became the lens through which Erdoğan viewed Turkish engagement with Operation Inherent Resolve. Yet this was to prove the source of immense tension with Ankara's NATO allies. Indeed the former US Defense Secretary Ash Carter argued that Turkey was the one nation, more than Russia and Iran, who 'caused the most complications for the campaign.'[46] The role played by the Kurdish People's Protection Units (YPG) in pushing ISIS out of the northern Iraqi town of Kobane in late 2014/early 2015 proved decisive in shifting American attitudes as to the utility of Kurdish militias as proxies and hardened Washington's opinion of an intransigent

Turkey.[47] Of all the external powers to intervene in Syria and Iraq, Turkey has had the most complicated war. Their implacable enemy, the Kurds, became a crucial ally for the West (even if they were eventually abandoned by President Trump's withdrawal announcement); ISIS terrorism has struck directly inside Turkey's borders, including two bomb attacks in Istanbul in 2016; internal political instability has been exacerbated by a huge influx of refugees; and Ankara's relationship with its NATO allies and its erstwhile partner Russia have reached a distinct nadir.

Turkish involvement in the war against ISIS got off to a slow start. The fall of Mosul in June 2014 that triggered the international response to ISIS proved to be a political crisis for Ankara after 49 staff members from the Turkish consulate in Mosul were held hostage for three months. The ensuing American assistance to embattled Kurdish groups in northern Iraq saw an important alliance emerge between the nascent Global Coalition and Turkey's erstwhile enemy, the Kurdish militias, all whilst Ankara remained paralysed in its response to ISIS.[48] Gains made by ISIS in Syria, especially into the Kurdish area around Kobane near the Turkish border in September 2014, did prompt Turkish troop movements. Although the Turkish parliament voted in favour of cross-border incursions if necessary to engage ISIS fighters, they proscribed Turkish forces from aiding Kurdish militias who were trying to defend Kurdish refugees. This prompted furious demonstrations of ethnic Kurds inside Turkey and left Turkey's standing amongst its allies and the Kurds 'in tatters'.[49]

In October 2014, shortly after Operation Inherent Resolve began, President Erdoğan set out four pre-conditions that would need to occur if Turkey were to increase its efforts: the introduction of a no-fly zone; a buffer zone inside Syria; the establishment of a training programme for anti-ISIS militias; and a targeting of the Assad regime in Syria.[50] Ankara's insistence on regime change in Damascus soon drove a wedge between Turkish strategy and that of its Western partners, who had come to see Assad's on-going position in power as a necessary evil to prevent complete state collapse in Syria.

One nation, however, found solace in the Turkish dilemma and helped create an alternative alliance that would try and undercut Iranian influence as well as expedite the removal of common enemy Assad: Saudi Arabia. The newly crowned King Salman agreed with Erdoğan during a meeting in Riyadh in March 2015 to initiate a weapons provision programme to selected opposition groups inside Syria. This agreement would see the Saudis provide TOW anti-tank missiles and other weaponry whilst the Turks facilitated their delivery across their border into Syria to its chosen proxy Jaysh al-Fath (The Army of Conquest).[51] When not collaborating with the Saudis to undermine Assad, Turkey's contribution to the fight against ISIS belatedly became focused on pushing them out of strongholds northeast of the Syrian city of Aleppo that stretched up to Turkish territory. 'Safe zones' were established on the Syrian side of the border for refugees to be protected by Turkish forces and for opposition forces to hold the line. The Turkish government proceeded with their own plans for this 'safe zone' even after the Obama administration requested that it be called the 'ISIS-free zone' as a reminder of who the real target was.[52]

As mentioned earlier in this chapter, the downing of a Russian fighter jet that had briefly strayed into Turkish airspace in November 2015 brought tensions between Ankara and Moscow to boiling point. With the Russians actively propping the Syrian regime up and the Turks actively agitating for its removal, the scene was set for reprisals. President Putin called the incident 'a stab in the back, carried out by the accomplices of terrorists', initiating a set of sanctions against Turkey and promising retaliatory action for any Turkish plane that ventured into Syrian airspace.[53] This effectively nullified the Turkish military influence inside northern Syria, allowing Kurdish groups like the YPG to cement their influence within the umbrella opposition group the Syrian Democratic Forces (SDF) and become a major force in the West's efforts to defeat ISIS on the ground. A partial rapprochement with the Russians by mid-2016 did allow Erdoğan to launch offensives against ISIS in the wake of two deadly ISIS attacks inside Turkey, one on the main airport in Istanbul in June, and the other on a wedding party in Gaziantep in August (perhaps it is also no coincidence that this show of force came a month after a failed coup against Erdoğan in Ankara). Operation Euphrates Shield saw Turkish special forces and selected proxies take on ISIS in a 15-mile corridor inside the Syrian border stretching from al-Ra'I to Jarabulus.

The issue of Kurdish fighters remained the most consistent source of tension between Erdoğan and leaders of the Global Coalition. American plans in January 2018 to train members of the 30,000-strong SDF, a Kurdish-dominated group, so that they could defend the Syrian side of the Turkish border was met with disgust in Ankara. President Erdoğan threatened to 'drown this terrorist force before it is born'.[54] He seemed to act on this promise because later the same month Turkey launched the ironically named Operation Olive Branch – an aerial campaign in Afrin province inside Syria targeting Kurdish militias. Airstrikes against the US-backed YPG were augmented by ground operations by Ankara's key proxy, the Syrian Free Army.[55] In the first month of Operation Olive Branch the Turkish Air Force used one-quarter of its entire fighter jet fleet in missions.[56]

Several months into Operation Olive Branch the Turkish Foreign Minister, Mevlüt Çavuşoğlu, lumped the PKK and YPG forces together with ISIS as representing what he called 'forces that exist only to pursue their dystopias'. He was keen for Turkey (who he pointed out was 'the only NATO ally to directly engage' terrorist forces with ground troops) to get significant credit for the rolling up of ISIS territory. He used an article in *Foreign Policy* to take aim at America's Kurdish proxies, arguing that Washington's actions in training and arming the YPG 'flies in the face of our alliance's values'. Çavuşoğlu branded the Kurdish militia training centres as 'terrorist encampments' that could be used 'to open a supplementary front for PKK terrorist operations' that could hollow out the space for a nascent Kurdish state.[57] Here lay the real rationale behind much of Turkey's positioning on ISIS and their lack of engagement, bordering on the deliberate stifling, of Operation Inherent Resolve. If Russia's intervention was really securing the position of Bashar al-Assad, then Turkey's was actually about retarding the forces of Kurdish nationalism.

In a strange twist Turkey's most influential contribution to the war against ISIS may have been in cementing President Trump's decision to withdraw US forces from Syria. In a phone call between Trump and Erdoğan two weeks before the US announcement in December 2018, the US president had been expected to warn his Turkish counterpart off continuing attacks against US-backed Kurdish militias – a standard line Washington had asked Ankara to tow since the beginning of the conflict. But, as reported by the Reuters news agency, during the call Trump was persuaded to abandon on-going American commitments and hand over to Turkey the job of 'finishing off Islamic State in Syria'.[58] A key consequence of the American withdrawal, alongside the green-lighting of greater Iranian influence regionally, is the abrogation of duties towards Kurdish fighters who had shouldered a massive burden in the ground war against ISIS. Trump has now abandoned them to the fate of Erdoğan for the sake of 'America First' isolationism.

## Conclusion

In an audacious diplomatic move in November 2017 President Putin invited his Iranian and Turkish counterparts to the Black Sea resort of Sochi to seek a peace plan for a post-ISIS Syria. This built upon their joint sponsorship of the first direct peace talks between the Assad regime and opposition groups in the Kazakh capital, Astana, earlier that year. The desire of this non-Western axis to shape the national, and possibly regional, landscape in and around Syria was evident in these talks that pointedly excluded any coalition partner nations. Discussions revolved around a possible new constitutional settlement and plans for a future presidential election.[59] The talks were designed to make a clear statement about who the powerbrokers in Syria really were, now that the threat from ISIS had been sufficiently diminished, and nearly all anti-Assad opposition groups tamed. It was a stark piece of *realpolitik* – one that not only minimised the role of the West in shaping the post-ISIS agenda but also essentially left Damascus as a hostage to the whims of Moscow and Tehran (Ankara, although at the table, had been successfully tamed by Moscow despite earlier tensions regarding the fate of the Assad regime). This will inevitably cause ructions further on down the line because whereas Iran's strategy in Syria appears to be based on weakening the state and creating parallel institutions loyal to Tehran, Russia's strategy is conversely based on the premise of strengthening the state and ensuring that loyalty to Moscow comes from the top down.[60]

All of this diplomatic engineering and its shrewd military deployment has resulted in Russia being a lynchpin in the war against ISIS[61] – even if its main objectives in Syria were not about retarding the group but about preserving Assad. The very size of its military commitment alone was a bold statement of intent, to the extent to which President Putin felt he could even mock the troop-free proxy war strategy of the West in a September 2015 speech to the UN General Assembly, stating that: 'any attempts to play games with terrorists, let alone to arm them, are not just short-sighted but fire hazardous [*sic*]'.[62]

The Global Coalition has not just been outmanoeuvred in Syria by Russia but actively stymied too. In October 2018, the outgoing Operation Inherent Resolve Deputy Commander, the British Major-General Felix Gedney, warned that the coalition was being outplayed by Russia, especially in the information domain: 'The Russians are really good at this, better than us … We saw a very clever, assiduous information campaign aimed at discrediting the campaign of the coalition'. Gedney cited 'a gaping vacuum in terms of the [campaign] narrative' that was filled by effective Russian information operations, including targeted photo opportunities of Russian troops delivering humanitarian aid in areas liberated from ISIS. In addition to these concerns the outgoing OIR commander, US Lieutenant General Paul Funk, cited extensive Russian electronic warfare as a constant nuisance to coalition activities, including electromagnetic jamming of US communications.[63]

As acute risk aversion came to dominate the American-led coalition response to ISIS, the calculated risk-taking of Russia and Iran has shifted the regional power balance and ensured that the campaign against ISIS has become a symbol of bigger geopolitical tensions that will continue to play out long after the end of Operation Inherent Resolve.

# Conclusion

## Operation Inherent Resolve and the Future of ISIS

The eventual retaking of Raqqa by Kurdish fighters from ISIS in October 2017 ensured that the nominal end of the caliphate occurred with a whimper not a bang. The rapidity of ISIS's demise was precipitous, its quasi-state bureaucratic structure dismantled, its territory lost, tens of thousands of its fighters dead, and its propaganda output diminished. Ultimately, ISIS was underdone by three key factors: the inability to succeed through continual conquest; the wedge driven between the group and local communities through acts of brutality in the name of law enforcement; and the effect of multiple military and paramilitary operations undertaken against it.[1] The contribution of Operation Inherent Resolve to the last of these three factors was limited.

On 1 May 2018, the coalition launched Operation Roundup, consisting of air and artillery strikes to support the Syrian Defence Force's (SDF) ground offensive against the remnants of ISIS in the Middle Euphrates River Valley.[2] By the beginning of the following year the military side of Operation Inherent Resolve had significantly wound down. Different coalition members began withdrawing their forces from the battlespace at different times. In April 2019, the French Army announced the imminent withdrawal of its 150-strong Wagram Task Force from the Iraq-Syria border region, stating that it had 'completed its mission' now ISIS was 'defeated'.[3] Despite this the coalition reiterated that even though the vast majority of ISIS territory had been recaptured, '[it] does not mean our campaign against ISIS is over'. It indicated that the coalition's four working groups – Foreign Terrorist Fighters; Counter-ISIS Financing; Communications; and Stabilisation – would continue to actively work towards the 'enduring defeat' of ISIS's 'trans-border networks, branches and affiliates'.[4] Yet the public statements cautioning against equating ISIS's territorial loss with an overall 'defeat' of the group were not mirrored in the pronouncements of individual leaders within the coalition. Many challenges still remain for coalition nations in the years ahead as ISIS looks to adapt. In this closing chapter it is pertinent to assess the dangers of viewing ISIS as a defeated group (especially in the era of the COVID-19 global health emergency), to evaluate the overall performance of the coalition in the war against ISIS thus far, and ponder the future of the group and where this might necessitate military responses in the years ahead.

## The dangers of the 'defeat' discourse and the implications of COVID-19

ISIS is not defeated because it is more than just a physical entity. It also represents an ideology whose worldview will push the group to reform elsewhere. The end of major combat operations against ISIS in Syria and Iraq will not be the end of the military campaign against the group. Operations inside their newly declared *wilayats* (provinces) in Africa, the Middle East, and Asia, will inevitably require more kill and capture missions to break up emergent cells who could prove more potent than their predecessors.[5] Moreover, this also requires Global Coalition members to offer continual security force assistance to nation-states vulnerable to new ISIS groupings.

In December 2017, the Iraqi prime minister, Haider al-Abadi, declared his nation's 'final victory' over ISIS, claiming that the recapturing of all Iraqi territory from them marked the end of the war against the group.[6] Incidentally, this announcement came just two days after the Russian military announced the defeat of ISIS in neighbouring Syria, on behalf of their ally Bashar al-Assad. The language of ISIS's 'defeat' did not begin with Donald Trump, but his loud pronouncements almost exactly a year later that ISIS was 'defeated' and therefore justified an American military withdrawal would have the most profound consequences.

It is hard to argue with *Washington Post* journalist Josh Rogin's assessment that Trump's withdrawal decision 'will saddle him with the sad distinction of taking a bad policy and turning it into a strategic blunder that will come back to haunt us'.[7] ISIS is down but not out. Even Trump's own Director of National Intelligence, Dan Coats, contradicted the president's assessment of a 'defeated' ISIS in a hearing before the Senate Intelligence Committee. He instead painted a picture of a group that would continue 'to stoke violence' in Syria. The US intelligence community's 2019 'Worldwide Threat Assessment', that Coats was giving testimony about, also acknowledged the on-going presence of thousands of ISIS fighters in Syria and Iraq and 12 known affiliate groups globally.[8] Even the former US special envoy to the Global Coalition, General John Allen, chimed in by warning that the growing ISIS presence in pockets of Africa, central and southeast Asia, mean that the geographical focus of the coalition's train and assist missions will need to shift in the years ahead.[9]

The fall of the caliphate's nominal 'capital', Raqqa, in October 2017 led many to write the obituary of ISIS. Robin Wright wrote that the group will be remembered as: 'a bizarre pseudo-state founded on illusory goals, created by a global horde of jihadis, and enforced with perverted viciousness [that] survived for three years, three months and some eighteen days'.[10] Yet the 'defeat' of ISIS is not yet upon us because, as Ben Taub has pointed out, 'the caliphate lives on as a fantasy of Islamic justice and governance which is measured against the corrupt reality of the Iraqi state'.[11] ISIS is a hybrid group that has simultaneously existed as a proto-state, an insurgency, and a terrorist network. The dismantling of the first component has not diminished the potency of the second and third elements.[12] As the Dutch National Coordinator for Security and Counter-Terrorism concluded in late 2018, the demise of the physical caliphate 'will not cease the mobilisation of ISIS's ideology. ISIS's eschatological message will remain intact and the power of the ISIS brand will probably be very slow to diminish'.[13] In a statement marking what it called 'the first anniversary of ISIS's territorial defeat', the Global Coalition itself warned that their work is 'far from complete as Daesh/ISIS remains a significant threat'.[14]

Further proof of the danger of the language of ISIS's 'defeat' is the Trump administration's pivot towards Iran. The fallout from the assassination of Qassem Soleimani has put the Global Coalition into a purely defensive posture at a precarious time at which 14,000 to 18,000 ISIS fighters still remain in Iraq and Syria.[15] Assuming the threat from ISIS is gone removes the only common issue that Washington and Tehran had a mutual interest in. An escalation in tensions is an inevitable consequence.

We must of course remember that the version of ISIS that was 'defeated' after its territory was lost and its leader killed is just the latest iteration of a group that under a previous guise also lost its strongholds (Iraq's Anbar province) and had a former leader killed (Abu Musab al-Zarqawi).[16] AQI was written off, yet it proved remarkably resilient and highly adaptive. The same mistake cannot be made in regard to ISIS.

Another reason that the defeat discourse is dangerous is the advantage that ISIS has taken of the COVID-19 global pandemic. In March 2020, as states around the world grappled to keep the virus under control, ISIS issued an editorial in its newsletter *Al-Naba* assuring supporters that COVID-19 would be no impediment to their actions. Importantly, it also instructed fighters to take advantage of the chaos caused by coronavirus and exploit the way in which the pandemic had become an all-consuming issue for all states in the Global Coalition. The piece in *Al-Naba* promised to turn this exploitative moment into 'the Crusader's worst nightmare'.[17]

With exquisite timing, just one day after the *Al-Naba* editorial appeared, the Combined Joint Task Force announced that all training missions for Operation Inherent Resolve with the Iraqi security forces were to be suspended, as well as the redeployment of many coalition troops back to their home nations. The coalition insisted that this 'repositioning' was the result of 'long-term planned adjustments to the force to reflect success in the campaign against Daesh and short-term moves to protect the force during the coronavirus pandemic'.[18] By the end of March 2020, the UK, Spain, Australia, France, Portugal, New Zealand, and the Netherlands had withdrawn nearly all their members of train, assist, and advise teams in the face of a two-month pause on operations announced by the Global Coalition.[19] US forces were relocated to smaller bases away from their forward operating bases, whilst the UK Ministry of Defence noted that the withdrawal of UK forces was part of a 'reduced requirement for training from the Iraqi Security Forces', who had been redeployed to major cities to police the strict COVID-19 curfews imposed by the government.[20] Some of the remaining US special forces operatives took social distancing to innovative new heights in May 2020 by resorting to drones to conduct training missions with Iraqi forces. The drones filmed Iraqi Army field exercises, which would then be reviewed by US personnel and feedback given via video conference.[21]

Admittedly, COVID-19 has sucked up a vast amount of political and economic capital in the West. Yet security threats of a non-epidemiological nature continue. The COVID-19 pandemic and its aftermath is a moment that could be exploited by violent non-state actors like ISIS with no interest in universal solidarity. It could buy them some vital planning and training time as the intensity of the anti-ISIS operations are scaled back. At the very least, this coronavirus-induced hiatus in operations against ISIS will grant the new leadership some space to reflect on strategic priorities and consider how to maximise the group's future capabilities. We have already witnessed an increase in attacks in villages in northern Iraq, including Khanaqin, Tuz Khurmath, and Amerli.[22] Such hyper-local activity could be construed as a village-by-village attempt at a reconstitution of lost territory. Furthermore, in this era of social distancing, it should be remembered that the pockets of ISIS resistance are already operating in small isolated groupings with limited access to the outside world – they are already, in the words of Michael Knight, the 'ultimate doomsday preppers'.[23] In parallel with the obvious weakening of the military resolve to keep operations ticking over, this is a dangerous time to conveniently buy in to the defeat discourse surrounding ISIS just because the pandemic response is monopolising Western political and security agendas.

## The death of al-Baghdadi and the future of ISIS

ISIS leader Abu Bakr al-Baghdadi's suicide in the Syrian town of Idlib to evade capture by US forces on 26 October 2019 marked the decapitation but not the ultimate defeat of the group. He had become a crucial symbolic target for the coalition amid the broader war against ISIS. He had come to embody, as ISIS propaganda never tired of repeating, the idea of an Islamic state. He put the caliph into caliphate. Even though he did not manage to issue a video communication for the vast majority of Operation Inherent Resolve, he remained a source of inspiration for the group.[24] More importantly, as *The Economist* pointed out after his death: 'the conditions that allowed it [ISIS] to rise – a region of corrupt, sectarian and ineffective governments that lord over poor, alienated populations – have, if anything, grown worse' since the group burst onto the scene in 2014.[25] It is exactly these conditions that the new ISIS leader, Amir Mohammed Abdul Rahman al-Mawli al-Salbi, will seek to exploit. Al-Salbi was a founding member of the group and played an instrumental role in enslaving the Yazidi population during the early years of the caliphate.[26]

Even with the talismanic al-Baghdadi dead, ISIS is still displaying crucial signs of life, including an ability to continue to draw on local resources where its remaining fighters hide out, its ability to demonstrate a form of bureaucratic functionality by setting up new *wilayats* in different regions, and a perpetuation of its ideological fanaticism through inspiring lone actor attacks globally. The future of ISIS is likely to look increasingly 'fragmented and atomized' as its international membership disperses to attach themselves to on-going civil wars, exploit insecure states, and plan more low-tech, mass-casualty attacks in the West.[27] This future iteration of the group will be impacted by its on-going rivalry with al-Qaeda, with the new ISIS leadership having to decide whether to continue vying for control of the global jihadist movement or consolidate their respective organisations in the spirit of jihadist *détente*. Intra-jihadist factionalism could be as debilitating to the group's regeneration as external military operations against it.

The residual threat of ISIS still remains in terms of money and personnel. Even when the last ISIS stronghold – the Syrian town of Baghuz – was holding out against advancing forces in March 2019, US officials acknowledged that the group still retained up to 20,000 fighters, with some forming sleeper cells ready to reactivate an insurgency at a later date.[28] This could be facilitated by the $400 million that is estimated to have been smuggled out of the caliphate before its collapse.[29] This looks to fit into a pattern of calculated strategic retreat, observable since their costly do-or-die defence of Mosul in July 2017. The deaths of thousands of ISIS fighters – who heeded Abu Bakr al-Baghdadi's plea to hold the city to the last man – was a watershed moment in the group's calculus. From then on, a large number of ISIS fighters noticeably decided to melt away rather than offer mortal resistance.[30] Journalist Mike Giglio spoke to ISIS fighters who, after the fall of Mosul, had paid people smugglers to get them over the border into Turkey – all with the blessing of their former commander who had ordered them to stay in Turkey until a future resurgence would necessitate their return.[31] This new approach of corporeal over territorial preservation indicates a reversion to a strategy of attrition, well adept to invoking a future insurgency.

After the eventual fall of Baghuz, al-Baghdadi released his first video message in five years in which he emphasised that the territory of the caliphate was not permanently lost but temporarily 'conquered'.[32] He was gearing his followers up for a long fight. Indeed, evidence suggests that even since the Iraqi government declared ISIS 'defeated' in late 2017, hundreds of attacks by ISIS loyalists have been perpetrated in areas thought to have been liberated from the group. This includes ambushing Iraqi security forces, assassinating dozens of village chiefs, and the planting of improvised explosive devices (IEDs) in parts of provinces like Anbar, Kirkuk, Diyala, and Salahaddin.[33] This reflects a return to the insurgent roots of many ISIS fighters, thousands of whom were trained in classic guerrilla tactics of hit-and-run, hiding within the population. Alongside a reversion to urban insurgency, other potential future strategic directions for ISIS include a relocation of its core activities to other unstable countries like Libya, and the linkage of existing franchises to build a global network.[34]

ISIS always was, and will remain, a hybrid threat that purveys unconventional warfare, terrorism, political activism, and religious extremism. Although the maintenance of a modern 'caliphate' has proven to be an abject failure, future leaders will inevitably play down the need to revamp such a grand ambition and instead calculate a more realistic, tactically astute set of goals.[35] Combine this with the continued presence of all the major themes that ISIS fed off in the first place – the corruption of local political leaders, pervasive Western political and military interference in the Middle East, and entrenched historical grievance within Sunni communities – and the ingredients for jihadist revanchism are all there.

## Assessing the performance of the Global Coalition and Operation Inherent Resolve

ISIS adopted an informal motto for its caliphate – *baqiya wa tatamaddad* ('lasting and expanding'). 'Short-lived and shrinking' might have made for a catchy, if not entirely appropriate, counter-narrative for Operation Inherent Resolve planners. Ensuring territorial loss became a key benchmark of coalition success as airstrikes and the efforts of various proxies on the ground were coordinated to help roll back areas of ISIS control.

Yet by many measures, Operation Inherent Resolve was a strange campaign with an oddly detached quality to it. As Mike Giglio puts it, in the war against ISIS:

> the only US soldiers on the front lines were the secret kind, small groups of commandos whose every mission was classified, while US pilots and drone operators dropped bombs. It was left to local soldiers ... to do the bulk of the fighting, and as far as most Americans and their politicians were concerned, the war was out of sight and out of mind.[36]

Unlike the previous iterations of the 'war on terror' in Iraq and Afghanistan, the absence of US military deaths in the thousands (indeed only 14 American soldiers died in the major combat phrase of Operation Inherent Resolve[37]) and the absence of major controversies over military conduct or rules of engagement infringements, left the US, and arguably most of its coalition allies, being peculiarly disconnected from the war itself. The ultimate sacrifice would be paid by Syrians, Kurds, and Iraqis opposing ISIS on the ground. For the West, ISIS was an immediate threat only truly in the context of domestic terror attacks by ISIS affiliates – London, Paris, Brussels, Manchester, Nice, San Bernadino, Orlando – but not in the context of foreign territorial gains – Mosul, Raqqa, Deir-e-Zor. The inter-connectivity of the fight inside the boundaries of the caliphate and internationally was evident in ISIS's strategic planning but not always necessarily in that of the West. Such strategic inertia resulted in Operation Inherent Resolve becoming, in the words of a RUSI report, 'a military operation to buy time', as political developments were (unsuccessfully) sought in Syria.[38] The operation remained 'inherently *un*resolved' as regional politics ignited a complex proxy war and long-term coalition strategy for the Assad regime in Damascus stymied decisive action.[39]

Strategic confusion was a hallmark of the coalition effort against ISIS. As a Congressional Research Service briefing in mid-2016 noted: 'Without a single authority responsible for prioritizing and adjudicating between different multinational civilian and military lines of effort, various actors often work at cross-purposes without intending to do so'. It also pointed to the 'different, often conflicting, longer-term regional geopolitical interests' that certain members of the coalition had to the US.[40] The early performance of Operation Inherent Resolve was 'disorganized and fragmented', as one Brookings Institute report put it, but began to gain a semblance of order under the command of General Sean McFarland, who took over in 2015.[41] Yet we must fundamentally appreciate that Operation Inherent Resolve was in itself a campaign designed as a corrective to the unintended consequences of Operation Iraqi Freedom. There was no al-Qaeda in Iraq until the US-led invasion in 2003. The original Bush-era War on Terror has spawned a non-stop set of subsequent campaigns needed to rectify the metastisation of the global jihadist movement that it was initially intent on retarding. The War on Terror is a bad movie that has produced numerous, equally unedifying sequels.

Yet it is a franchise that shows no signs of ending because the coalition is still facing a set of issues that will need resolving in the years ahead. One of the most pressing strategic issues left unresolved by the coalition is a political one – namely the failure to build a moderate Sunni faction within the broader Iraqi and Syrian body politic.[42] This failure is important because the vacuum left in former ISIS-controlled territory has been filled by Shia, not Sunni groups, including the national Iraqi security forces (who are mainly Shia), Shia militias that are controlled to some degree by Iran, not to mention other non-Sunni factions including the Kurds and Turkish or Russian military personnel.

Another hugely important problem facing the coalition in the years to come is the issue of returning foreign fighters – and indeed the women who travelled to the caliphate to marry them. Yesterday's security threat abroad could become tomorrow's security threat at home. Rehabilitation and reintegration schemes need therefore to be effectively implemented, above and beyond the innate political desire to simply imprison.

Due to the fact that tackling ISIS is as much about defeating their ideas as it is about reducing their paramilitary threat, the war against them is not over yet. Regardless of changes of leadership or the absence of a proto-state to continue calling their own, ISIS is still a potent symbol to its sympathisers. It retains the ability to recruit, the capacity to radicalise, and the capability to reform. Coalition military action may be winding down but ISIS will continue to fight for relevance at this strategically vulnerable time by claiming responsibility for the terrorist actions of lone actors it has no control over as well as continuing to exploit security vacuums in unstable areas around the world. As the evolution of jihadist violence continues apace, the strategic response to its next iteration must be more robust and more coherent than Operation Inherent Resolve.

# Notes

## Introduction

1    Colin P. Clarke, *After the Caliphate: The Islamic State and the Future of the Terrorist Diaspora* (Cambridge: Polity, 2019), pp. 41 and 50.

2    BBC News, 'Islamic State group "lost quarter of territory" in 2016', 19 January 2017, http://www.bbc.co.uk/news/world-middle-east-38641509

3    Falih Hassan and Rod Nordland, 'Battered ISIS keeps grip on last piece of territory for over a year', *The New York Times*, 9 December 2018, https://www.nytimes.com/2018/12/09/world/middleeast/isis-territory-syria-iraq.html

4    For example, see Charles Lister, *The Syrian Jihad: Al-Qaeda, the Islamic State and the Evolution of an Insurgency* (London: Hurst, 2015); Will McCants, *The ISIS Apocalypse: The History, Strategy, and Doomsday Vision of the Islamic State* (New York: St. Martin's Press, 2015); Michael Weiss and Hassan Hassan, *ISIS: Inside the Army of Terror* (New York: Regan Arts, 2015); and Jessica Stern and J.M Berger, *ISIS: State of Terror* (London: William Collins, 2015).

5    For example, see Peter R. Neumann, *Radicalized: New Jihadists and the Threat to the West* (London: I.B. Tauris, 2016); Paul Gill, *Lone Actor Terrorists: A Behavioural Analysis* (Abingdon: Routledge, 2016); and Jeffrey Simon, *Lone Wolf Terrorism: Understanding the Growing Threat* (Buffalo, NY: Prometheus Books, 2016).

6    For example, see Rajiv Chandrasekaran, *Little America: The War within the War for Afghanistan* (London: Bloomsbury, 2013); Seth Jones, *In the Graveyard of Empires: America's War in Afghanistan* (New York: Norton, 2009); Theo Farrell, *Unwinnable: Britain's War in Afghanistan, 2001–2014* (London: Bodley Head, 2017); Carter Malkesian, *War Comes to Garmser* (London: Hurst, 2016).

7    For example, see Michael Gordon and Bernard Trainor, *Cobra II: The Inside Story of the Invasion and Occupation of Iraq* (London: Atlantic

Books, 2006); Thomas Ricks, *Fiasco: The American Military Adventure in Iraq* (London: Penguin, 2006); Thomas Ricks, *The Gamble: General David Petraeus and the American Military Adventure in Iraq* (New York: Allen Lane, 2009); Linda Robinson, *Tell Me How This Ends: General David Petraeus and the Search for a Way Out of Iraq* (New York: Public Affairs, 2008); Ahmed S. Hashim, *Insurgency and Counter-Insurgency in Iraq* (London: Hurst, 2006); Ali A. Allawi, *The Occupation of Iraq: Winning the War, Losing the Peace* (New Haven, CT: Yale University Press, 2007).

8   Remarks of President Obama and President Ilves of Estonia in Joint Press Conference, 3 September 2014, https://obamawhitehouse.archives. gov/the-press-office/2014/09/03/remarks-president-obama-and-president-ilves-estonia-joint-press-confer-0

9   Hussein Bana, 'International and Regional Responses: An Appraisal', in Faisal al-Istrabadi and Sumit Ganguly (eds.), *The Future of ISIS: Regional and International Implications* (Washington, DC: Brookings Institution Press, 2018), p. 164.

10  Daniel Byman, 'ISIS Goes Global', *Foreign Affairs*, Vol. 95, No. 2 (2016), pp. 76–85.

## 1  The Rise of ISIS and the Creation of the Coalition

1   Mary Anne Weaver, 'The short, violent life of Abu Musab al-Zarqawi', *The Atlantic*, July/August 2006, https://www.theatlantic.com/magazine/ archive/2006/07/the-short-violent-life-of-abu-musab-al-zarqawi/304983/

2   Colin P. Clarke, *After the Caliphate: The Islamic State and the Future of the Terrorist Diaspora* (Cambridge: Polity, 2019), pp. 57–58.

3   Clarke, *After the Caliphate*, p. 62.

4   Charles Lister, 'Profiling the Islamic State' (Washington, DC: Brookings Institute, December 2014), https://www.brookings.edu/research/ profiling-the-islamic-state/, p. 2.

5   Graeme Wood, 'What ISIS really wants', *The Atlantic*, March 2015, http://www.theatlantic.com/features/archive/2015/02/what-isis-really-wants/384980

6   Gareth Stansfield, 'Explaining the Aims, Rise, and Impact of the Islamic State in Iraq and al-Sham', *The Middle East Journal*, Vol. 70, No. 1 (2016), pp. 148–49.

7   Ben Fishman, 'Defining ISIS', *Survival*, Vol. 58, No. 1 (2016), p. 180.

8   James Fromson and Steven Simon, 'ISIS: The Dubious Paradise of Apocalypse Now', *Survival*, Vol. 57, No. 3 (2015), p. 8.

9   Richard English, 'The ISIS Crisis', *Journal of Terrorism Research*, Vol. 8, No. 1 (2017), p. 90.

10  Dan Byman, 'Understanding the Islamic State: A Review Essay', *International Security*, Vol. 40, No. 4 (2016), p. 129.

11  Clarke, *After the Caliphate*, p. 2.

12  Craig Whiteside, 'The Islamic State and the Return of Revolutionary Warfare', *Small Wars and Insurgencies*, Vol. 27, No. 5 (2016), p. 744.

13  Tom Stevenson, 'How to run a Caliphate', *London Review of Books*, 20 June 2019, https://www.lrb.co.uk/the-paper/v41/n12/tom-stevenson/how-to-run-a-caliphate

14  Nadia Al-Dayel, Andrew Mumford, and Kevin Bales, 'Not Yet Dead': The Establishment and Regulation of Slavery by the Islamic State', *Studies in Conflict and Terrorism*, https://www.tandfonline.com/doi/full/10.1080/1057610X.2020.1711590

15  For a detailed assessment of ISIS's treatment of women, see Azadeh Moaveni, *Guest House for Young Widows: Among the Women of ISIS* (London: Scribe, 2019).

16  'Kerry, Hagel Joint Statement on ISIL Meeting with Key Partners', US Embassy in Syria press release, 5 September 2014, https://sy.usembassy.gov/kerry-hagel-joint-statement-isil-meeting-key-partners/

17  Congressional Research Service (CRS), 'Coalition Contributions to Countering the Islamic State', 24 August 2016, https://fas.org/sgp/crs/natsec/R44135.pdf

18  US Department of State, 'Joint Statement issued by partners at the Counter-ISIL Coalition Ministerial Meeting', 3 December 2014, https://2009-2017.state.gov/r/pa/prs/ps/2014/12/234627.htm

19  Combined Joint Task Force – Operation Inherent Resolve (CJTF-OIR) website, 'Campaign Design', https://www.inherentresolve.mil/campaign/

20  Ibid.

21  John R. Allen, 'I was special envoy to fight the Islamic State. Our gains are now at risk', *The Washington Post*, 3 January 2019, https://www. washingtonpost.com/opinions/i-was-special-envoy-to-fight-the-islamic-state-trump-could-unravel-our-gains/2019/01/03/2339f1a4-0ebe-11e9-84fc-d58c33d6c8c7_story.html?noredirect=on&utm_term=.90099ff98b23

22  Kenneth M. Pollack, 'Iraq Situation Report, Part I: The Military Campaign Against ISIS' (Washington, DC: Brookings Institute, 28 March 2016), https://www.brookings.edu/blog/markaz/2016/03/28/iraq-situation-report-part-i-the-military-campaign-against-isis/

23  'Letter to D-ISIS Coalition Partners on the Progress of the Past Year', Brett McGurk, Special Presidential Envoy for the Global Coalition to Counter ISIS, 29 December 2017, https://www.state.gov/s/seci/2017remarks/276806.htm

24  'Coalition announces shift in focus as Iraq campaign progresses', Combined Joint Task Force Operation Inherent Resolve news release, 5 February 2018, https://dod.defense.gov/News/Article/Article/1432692/coalition-announces-shift-in-focus-as-iraq-campaign-progresses/

25  Pollack, 'Iraq Situation Report, Part I'.

26  Peter Baker, 'A coalition in which some do more than others to fight ISIS', *The New York Times*, 29 November 2015, https://www.nytimes.com/2015/11/30/us/politics/a-coalition-in-which-some-do-more-than-others-to-fight-isis.html

27  Aaron Mehta, 'Carter again slams anti-ISIS partners on lack of assistance', *Defense News*, 2 February 2016, https://www.defensenews.com/pentagon/2016/02/02/carter-again-slams-anti-isis-partners-on-lack-of-assistance/

28  Ash Carter, 'A Lasting Defeat: The Campaign to Destroy ISIS', Belfer Center special report (October 2017), p. 41, https://www.belfercenter.org/LastingDefeat

29  For example, see Andrew Mumford, *Counter-Insurgency Warfare and the Anglo-American Alliance: The 'Special Relationship' on the Rocks* (Washington, DC: Georgetown University Press, 2017); and David P. Auerswald and Stephen M. Saideman, *NATO in Afghanistan: Fighting Together, Fighting Alone* (Princeton, NJ: Princeton University Press, 2014).

30  Quoted in Joby Warrick, *Black Flags: The Rise of ISIS* (London: Corgi Books, 2016), p. 35.

31  Fredrik Doeser, 'Historical Experiences, Strategic Culture, and Strategic Behaviour: Poland in the Anti-ISIS Coalition', *Defence Studies*, Vol. 18, No. 4 (2018), p. 454.

32  For a full breakdown of the data and analysis, see Tim Haesebrouck, 'Democratic Participation in the Air Strikes Against Islamic State: A Qualitative Comparative Analysis', *Foreign Policy Analysis*, Vol. 14, No. 2 (2018), pp. 254–75.

33  Linda Robinson, 'Assessment of the Politico-Military Campaign to Counter ISIL and Options for Adaptation', RAND Corporation report (Santa Monica, CA: RAND, 2016), p. 1, https://www.rand.org/pubs/research_reports/RR1290.html; Tim Lister, 'A Frontline Report: The Ground War Against the Islamic State', *CTC Sentinel*, Vol. 8, Issue 11 (November/December 2015), p. 13, https://ctc.usma.edu/a-frontline-report-the-ground-war-against-the-islamic-state/

34  Geraint Alun Hughes, 'Syria and the Perils of Proxy Warfare', *Small Wars and Insurgencies*, Vol. 25, No. 3 (2014), p. 525.

35  BBC News, 'US and UK suspend non-lethal aid for Syria rebels', 11 December 2013, http://www.bbc.co.uk/news/world-middle-east-25331241

36  Ian Cobain, Alice Ross, Rob Evans, and Mona Mahmood, 'How Britain funds the "propaganda war" against ISIS in Syria', *The Guardian*, 3 May 2016, http://www.theguardian.com/world/2016/may/03/how-britain-funds-the-propaganda-war-against-isis-in-syria

37  Anthony Seldon and Peter Snowden, *Cameron at 10: The Verdict* (London: William Collins, 2016), pp. 463–70.

38  House of Commons Library briefing paper #8248, 'ISIS/Daesh: What Now for the Military Campaign in Iraq and Syria?', 7 March 2018, p. 7, https://researchbriefings.parliament.uk/ResearchBriefing/Summary/CBP-8248#fullreport

39  Australian Strategic Policy Institute (APSI), 'Strike from the Air: The First 100 Days of the Campaign Against ISIL' (December 2014), p. 7, https://www.aspi.org.au/report/strike-air-first-100-days-campaign-against-isil

40  Fredrik Doeser and Joackim Eidenfalk, 'Using Strategic Culture to Understand Participation in Expeditionary Operations: Australia, Poland, and the Coalition Against the Islamic State', *Contemporary Security Policy*, Vol. 40, No. 1 (2019), p. 13.

41  Quoted in Alissa J. Rubin and Anne Barnard, 'France strikes ISIS targets in Syria in retaliation for attacks', *The New York Times*, 15 November 2015, https://www.nytimes.com/2015/11/16/world/europe/paris-terror-attack.html

## 2  America's War – From 'Degrade and Destroy' to the 'Defeat' of ISIS

1  Center for a New American Security (CNAS), 'Defeating the Islamic State: A Bottom-Up Approach' (June 2016), p. 4, https://www.cnas.org/publications/reports/defeating-the-islamic-state-a-bottom-up-approach

2  J.M. Berger, 'Barack Obama still misunderestimates ISIL', *Politico*, 22 May 2015, https://www.politico.com/magazine/story/2015/05/barack-obama-still-misunderestimates-isil-118204

3  US Department of Defense, Operation Inherent Resolve' website, https://dod.defense.gov/OIR/

4  David Kilcullen, *Blood Year: Islamic State and the Failures of the War on Terror* (London: Hurst, 2016), p. 95.

5  Ben Rhodes, *The World As It Is: Inside Obama's White House* (London: Bodley Head, 2018), p. 291.

6  Anthony H. Cordesman, 'The Islamic State War: No Clear US Strategy', Center for Strategic and International Studies (CSIS) research paper (November 2014), p. 4, https://www.csis.org/analysis/islamic-state-war-no-clear-us-strategy

7  James Fromson and Steven Simon, 'ISIS: The Dubious Paradise of Apocalypse Now', *Survival*, Vol. 57, No. 3 (2015), p. 7.

8  Rhodes, *The World As It Is*, p. 291.

9  James S. Robbins, 'Fighting the Islamic State: The US Scorecard', *Journal of International Security Studies*, No. 30 (Winter 2016), http://www.securityaffairs.org/issues/number-30/fighting-the-islamic-state-us-scorecard

10  Ash Carter, 'A Lasting Defeat: The Campaign to Destroy ISIS', Belfer Center special report (October 2017), p. 12, https://www.belfercenter.org/LastingDefeat

11  Cordesman, 'The Islamic State War', p. 3.

12  Quoted in Jeffrey Goldberg, 'The Obama doctrine', *The Atlantic*, April 2016, https://www.theatlantic.com/magazine/archive/2016/04/the-obama-doctrine/471525/

13  Jessica Stern, "Obama and Terrorism", *Foreign Affairs*, Vol. 94 (September/October 2015), p. 64, https://www.foreignaffairs.com/articles/obama-and-terrorism

14  'Statement by the President', White House, 7 August 2014, https://obamawhitehouse.archives.gov/the-press-office/2014/08/07/statement-president

15  'Statement by the President on ISIL', White House, 10 September 2014, https://obamawhitehouse.archives.gov/the-press-office/2014/09/10/statement-president-isil-1

16  Ibid.

17  Carter, 'A Lasting Defeat', pp. 5–6.

18  Ibid., p. 18.

19  Ibid., pp. 8–9.

20  Department of Defense press release, '1 year in: officials assess anti-ISIL progress', 6 August 2015, https://www.defense.gov/Explore/News/Article/Article/612754/1-year-in-officials-assess-anti-isil-progress/

21  Statistics quoted in Peter R. Neumann, *Bluster: Donald Trump's War on Terror* (London: Hurst, 2019), p. 99.

22  Neumann, *Bluster*, p. 3.

23  John Bew and Shiraz Maher, 'Syria's World War', *New Statesman*, 11 April 2018, https://www.newstatesman.com/world/middle-east/2018/04/syria-assad-trump-war-britain-us-strike-russia

24  Charles Lister and William F. Wechsler, 'Trump has big plans for Syria, but he has no real strategy', *Politico*, 20 January 2018, https://www.politico.com/magazine/story/2018/01/30/donald-trump-syria-strategy-216551

25  Neumann, *Bluster*, p. 108.

26  Quoted in Michael Wolff, *Fire and Fury: Inside the Trump White House* (London: Little, Brown, 2018), p. 7.

27 Mike Giglio, *Shatter the Nations: ISIS and the War for the Caliphate* (New York: Public Affairs, 2019), p.241.

28 Presidential Memorandum, 'Plan to Defeat the Islamic State of Iraq and Syria', 28 January 2017, https://www.whitehouse.gov/presidential-actions/presidential-memorandum-plan-defeat-islamic-state-iraq-syria/

29 Kori Schake, 'Rex Tillerson's Syria policy is sensible – but it's fanciful', *The Atlantic*, 18 January 2018, https://www.theatlantic.com/international/archive/2018/01/tillerson-syria-stanford/550853/

30 Quoted in Lister and Wechsler, 'Trump has big plans for Syria'.

31 BBC News, 'Syria conflict: US officials withdraw troops after IS "defeat"', 19 December 2018, https://www.bbc.co.uk/news/world-middle-east-46623617

32 Josh Rogin, 'Trump undermines his entire national security team on Syria', *The Washington Post*, 19 December 2018, https://www.washingtonpost.com/opinions/2018/12/19/trump-undermines-his-entire-national-security-team-syria/

33 BBC News, 'Syria conflict'.

34 US National Security Strategy, Washington, DC, December 2017, p. 11, https://www.whitehouse.gov/wp-content/uploads/2017/12/NSS-Final-12-18-2017-0905.pdf

35 Quoted in Jeff Schogol, 'Mattis says Syria policy has not changed after White House changes Syria policy', *Task and Purpose*, 24 September 2018, https://taskandpurpose.com/mattis-says-no-syria-policy-changes

36 Quoted in W.J. Hennigan, '"I was not consulted": Top US general left out of Syria withdrawal decision', *TIME Magazine*, 5 February 2019, https://time.com/5521419/syria-withdrawal-donald-trump-joseph-votel/

37 Rogin, 'Trump undermines his entire national security team on Syria'.

38 Quoted in Richard Engel and Kennett Werner, 'White House chaos jeopardizes war on ISIS, US commanders warn', NBC News, 20 March 2018, https://www.nbcnews.com/news/world/white-house-chaos-jeopardizes-war-isis-u-s-commanders-warn-n859966

39 Quoted in Julian Borger, 'Defense Secretary James Mattis resigns and points to differences with Trump', *The Guardian*, 21 December 2018,

https://www.theguardian.com/us-news/2018/dec/20/jim-mattis-defense-secretary-retires-trump

40  Quoted in Rukmini Callimachi and Eric Schmitt, 'Splitting with Trump over Syria, American leading ISIS fight steps down', *The New York Times*, 22 December 2018, https://www.nytimes.com/2018/12/22/world/brett-mcgurk-isis-resign.html

41  Peter W. Galbraith, 'The betrayal of the Kurds', *The New York Review of Books*, 21 November 2019, https://www.nybooks.com/articles/2019/11/21/betrayal-of-the-kurds/

## 3  The Proxy Wars For and Against ISIS

1  Andrew Mumford, *Proxy Warfare* (Cambridge: Polity, 2013), p. 1.

2  David Ignatius, 'Foreign nations' proxy war in Syria creates chaos', *The Washington Post*, 2 October 2014, http://www.washingtonpost.com/opinions/david-ignatius-foreign-nations-proxy-war-creates-syrian-chaos/2014/10/02/061fb50c-4a7a-11e4-a046-120a8a855cca_story.html

3  Ibid.

4  Patrick Cockburn, *The Rise of Islamic State: ISIS and the New Sunni Revolution* (London: Verso, 2015), p. 159

5  Stephen S. Saideman, 'The Ambivalent Coalition: Doing the Least One Can Do Against the Islamic State', *Contemporary Security Policy*, Vol. 37, No. 2 (2016), p. 290.

6  Remarks of President Obama and President Ilves of Estonia in Joint Press Conference, 3 September 2014, https://obamawhitehouse.archives.gov/the-press-office/2014/09/03/remarks-president-obama-and-president-ilves-estonia-joint-press-confer-0

7  Graeme Wood, 'What ISIS really wants', *The Atlantic*, March 2015, http://www.theatlantic.com/features/archive/2015/02/what-isis-really-wants/384980

8  Will McCants, *The ISIS Apocalypse: The History, Strategy, and Doomsday Vision of the Islamic State* (New York: St. Martin's Press, 2015), p.156.

9   Quoted in Thomas L. Friedman, 'Obama on the world', *The New York Times*, 8 August 2014, https://www.nytimes.com/2014/08/09/opinion/president-obama-thomas-l-friedman-iraq-and-world-affairs.html

10  Tyrone L. Groh, *Proxy War: The Least Bad Option* (Stanford, CA: Stanford University Press, 2019).

11  Ignatius, 'Foreign nations' proxy war in Syria creates chaos'.

12  Cockburn, *The Rise of Islamic State*, pp. 85–86.

13  BBC News, 'UK to give military training to "moderate Syria forces"', 26 March 2015, http://www.bbc.co.uk/news/uk-32064130

14  Joby Warrick, *Black Flags: The Rise of ISIS* (London: Corgi Books, 2016), pp. 380–82.

15  Charles Lister, *The Syrian Jihad: Al-Qaeda, the Islamic State and the Evolution of an Insurgency* (London: Hurst, 2015), p. 217.

16  Greg Miller, 'CIA ramping up covert training program for moderate Syrian rebels', *The Washington Post*, 2 October 2013, https://www.washingtonpost.com/world/national-security/cia-ramping-up-covert-training-program-for-moderate-syrian-rebels/2013/10/02/a0bba084-2af6-11e3-8ade-a1f23cda135e_story.html?utm_term=.3ab61eed5d2d

17  Charles Lister, 'The Free Syrian Army: A Decentralized Insurgent Brand', Brookings Project on US Relations with the Islamic World Analysis Paper #26 (November 2016), pp. 34–38, https://www.brookings.edu/research/the-free-syrian-army-a-decentralized-insurgent-brand/

18  Ibid., pp. 3–13.

19  Warrick, *Black Flag*, p. 372.

20  David Kilcullen, *Blood Year: Islamic State and the Failures of the War on Terror* (London: Hurst, 2016), p. 79.

21  BBC News, 'Assad says Syria is informed on anti-IS air campaign', 10February 2015, http://www.bbc.co.uk/news/world-middle-east-31312414

22  Cockburn, *The Rise of Islamic State*, p. 92.

23  Michael Weiss and Hassan Hassan, *ISIS: Inside the Army of Terror* (New York: Regan Arts, 2015), pp. 99–102.

24  Ibid., p. 219.

25  Quoted in Weiss and Hassan, *ISIS*, p. 221.

26   Helene Cooper, 'Obama requests money to train "appropriately vetted" Syrian rebels', *The New York Times*, 26 June 2014, www.nytimes.com/2014/06/27/world/middleeast/obama-seeks-500-million-to-train-and-equip-syrian-opposition.html

27   David Remnick, 'Going the distance', *The New Yorker*, 27 January 2014, www.newyorker.com/magazine/2014/01/27/going-the-distance-david-remnick

28   Andreas Krieg, 'Externalizing the Burden of War: The Obama Doctrine and US Foreign Policy in the Middle East', *International Affairs*, Vol. 92, No. 1 (2016), p. 97.

29   House Joint Resolution 124, Continuing Appropriations Resolution #2,015, 113th Congress (2013–14), https://www.congress.gov/bill/113th-congress/house-joint-resolution/124

30   BBC News, 'US campaign against Islamic State in Syria "intensifying"', 7 July 2015, http://www.bbc.co.uk/news/world-middle-east-33418021

31   Spencer Ackerman, 'US has trained only "four or five" Syrian fighters against ISIS, top general testifies', *The Guardian*, 16 September 2015, https://www.theguardian.com/us-news/2015/sep/16/us-military-syrian-isis-fighters

32   Quoted in Eric Schmitt and Ben Hubbard, 'US revamping rebel force fighting ISIS in Syria', *The New York Times*, 6 September 2015, http://www.nytimes.com/2015/09/07/world/middleeast/us-to-revamp-training-program-to-fight-isis.html

33   Steve Ferenzi, 'Beyond Half Measures: Influencing Syria's Political Order through Non-state Proxies', *Small Wars Journal*, May 2016, https://smallwarsjournal.com/jrnl/art/beyond-half-measures-influencing-syria's-political-order-through-non-state-proxies (emphasis added).

34   Mike Giglio, 'America is in a proxy war with itself in Syria', *Buzzfeed News*, 20 February 2016, http://www.buzzfeed.com/mikegiglio/america-is-now-fighting-a-proxy-war-with-itself-in-syria?htm_term=.pya4DXoBb#.gkrErY4k2

35   Kilcullen, *Blood Year*, p. 105 (original emphasis).

36   For a good overview of the emergence of the Western-Kurdish proxy alliance in 2014–15, see Rod Thornton, 'Problems with the Kurds as

Proxies Against Islamic State: Insights from the Siege of Kobane', *Small Wars and Insurgencies*, Vol. 26, No. 6 (2015), pp. 865–85.

37  Quoted in Joe Parkinson and Dion Nissenbaum, 'US allies training Kurds on using sophisticated weaponry against Islamic State', *The Wall Street Journal*, 21 September 2014, http://www.wsj.com/articles/U-S-allies -training-kurds-on-using-islamic-state-1411339625

38  Kilcullen, *Blood Year*, pp. 138, 157.

39  UK Ministry of Defence press release, 'UK provides further equipment to Kurdish fighters tackling ISIL', 22 June 2015, https://www.gov.uk/government/news/uk-provides-further-equipment-to-kurdish-fighters-tackling-isil

40  BBC News, 'Germany to supply arms to Kurds fighting IS in Iraq', 1 September 2014, https://www.bbc.co.uk/news/world-europe-29012159

41  Danish Institute for International Studies policy brief, 'A Difficult Balancing Act: Backing the Kurds in the Fight Against IS in Iraq and Syria' (November 2014), https://pure.diis.dk/ws/files/632411/diis_pb_backing_the_kurds_print.pdf

42  Reuters, 'Exclusive: US commanders recommend letting Kurdish fighters in Syria keep weapons', 28 December 2018, https://uk.reuters.com/article/uk-mideast-crisis-syria-usa-exclusive/exclusive-u-s-commanders-recommend-letting-kurdish-fighters-in-syria-keep-weapons-idUKKCN1OR1OH

43  Malise Ruthven, 'How to understand ISIS', *The New York Review of Books*, 23 June 2016, https://www.nybooks.com/articles/2016/06/23/how-to-understand-isis/

44  Mark Mazzetti, Anne Barnard, and Eric Schmitt, 'Military success in Syria gives Putin upper hand in US proxy war', *The New York Times*, 6 August 2016, http://www.nytimes.com/2016/08/07/world/middleeast/military-syria-putin-us-proxy-war.html

45  Andrew Mumford, 'Proxy Warfare and the Future of Conflict', *RUSI Journal*, Vol. 158, No. 2 (2013), p. 45.

46  Quoted in Ruthven, 'How to understand ISIS'.

47  Mark Mazzetti, Adam Goldman, and Michael S. Schmidt, 'Behind the sudden death of a $1billion secret CIA war in Syria', *New York Times*,

2 August 2017, https://www.nytimes.com/2017/08/02/world/
middleeast/cia-syria-rebel-arm-train-trump.html

48  Cockburn, *The Rise of Islamic State*, p. 3.

49  BBC News, 'Islamic State: US probes "stray Syria air drop" in IS video',
22 October 2014, http://www.bbc.co.uk/news/world-middle-east-
29715044

50  Conflict Armament Research, 'Weapons of the Islamic State' (December
2017), https://www.conflictarm.com/weapons-of-the-islamic-state/

51  Ruth Sherlock, 'Syrian rebels armed and trained by US surrendered to
al-Qaeda', *The Telegraph*, 2 November 2014, http://www.telegraph.co.uk/
news/worldnews/middleeast/syria/11203825/Syrian-rebels-armed-and-
trained-by-US-surrender-to-al-Qaeda.html

52  Quote in Jeff Stein, 'Inside the CIA's Syrian rebels vetting machine',
*Newsweek*, 21 November 2014, https://www.newsweek.com/2014/11/21/
moderate-rebels-please-raise-your-hands-283449.html

53  Steve Clemons, '"Thank God for the Saudis": ISIS, Iraq, and the lessons of
blowback', *The Atlantic*, 23 June 2014, http://theatlantic.com/international/
archive/2014/06/isis-saudi-arabia-iraq-syria-bandar/373181

54  BBC News, 'Qatar officials dismiss IS funding claims', 27 October 2014,
http://www.bbc.co.uk/news/world-middle-east-29782291

55  Ibid.

56  Mark Mazzetti and Matt Apuzzo, 'US relies heavily on Saudi money to
support Syrian rebels', *The New York Times*, 23 January 2016, https://
www.nytimes.com/2016/01/24/world/middleeast/us-relies-heavily-on-
saudi-money-to-support-syrian-rebels.html

57  Kilcullen, *Blood Year*, p. 105.

58  Weiss and Hassan, *ISIS*, p. 144.

59  Ibid., p. 144.

60  BBC News, 'Turkey's downing of Russian warplane – what we know',
1 December 2015, https://www.bbc.co.uk/news/world-middle-
east-34912581

61  Austin Carson and Michael Poznansky, 'The Logic for (Shoddy) US
Covert Action in Syria', *War on the Rocks*, 21 July 2016, https://
warontherocks.com/2016/07/the-logic-for-shoddy-u-s-covert-action-
in-syria/

62  Quoted in International Crisis Group, 'Arming Iraq's Kurds: Fighting IS, Inviting Conflict', *Middle East Report*, No. 158 (12 May 2015), p. 18, https://www.crisisgroup.org/middle-east-north-africa/gulf-and-arabian-peninsula/iraq/arming-iraq-s-kurds-fighting-inviting-conflict

63  Jessica Stern and J.M. Berger, *ISIS: State of Terror* (London: William Collins, 2015), p. 254.

64  C. Anthony Pffaf and Patrick Granfield, 'How (not) to fight proxy wars', *The National Interest*, 27 March 2018, https://nationalinterest.org/feature/how-not-fight-proxy-wars-25102

65  Patrick Martin and Christopher Kozak, 'The Pitfalls of Relying on Kurdish Forces in Counter ISIS' (Washington, DC: Institute for the Study of War, February 2016), http://www.understandingwar.org/backgrounder/pitfalls-relying-kurdish-forces-counter-isis-0

66  Inaugural Address of President Donald J. Trump, 20 January 2017, https://www.whitehouse.gov/inaugural-address

67  Krieg, 'Externalizing the Burden of War', p. 97.

## 4  On the Ground and in the Air – Assessing the Special Forces Operations, Local Force Training Missions, and Aerial Campaign Against ISIS

1  Daniel Byman and Ian A. Merritt, 'The New American Way of War: Special Operations Forces in the War on Terrorism', *Washington Quarterly*, Vol. 41, No. 2 (2018), pp. 79, 83.

2  Ibid., p. 83

3  Ibid., p. 83.

4  David Kilcullen, *Blood Year: Islamic State and the Failures of the War on Terror* (London: Hurst, 2016), p. 96.

5  Ibid., p. 96.

6  Linda Robinson, 'Assessment of the Politico-Military Campaign to Counter ISIL and Options for Adaptation', RAND Corporation report (Santa Monica, CA: RAND, 2016), p. 29, https://www.rand.org/pubs/research_reports/RR1290.html

7   Robert H. Scales, 'The only way to defeat the Islamic State', *The Washington Post*, 5 September 2014, https://www.washingtonpost.com/opinions/the-only-way-to-defeat-the-islamic-state/2014/09/05/4b2d7bd4-3459-11e4-a723-fa3895a25d02_story.html

8   Ash Carter, 'A Lasting Defeat: The Campaign to Destroy ISIS', Belfer Center special report (October 2017), p. 29, https://www.belfercenter.org/LastingDefeat

9   Helene Cooper and Eric Schmitt, 'ISIS official killed in US raid in Syria, Pentagon says', *The New York Times*, 16 May 2015, https://www.nytimes.com/2015/05/17/world/middleeast/abu-sayyaf-isis-commander-killed-by-us-forces-pentagon-says.html

10   Ben Farmer, 'SAS "took part in Abu Sayyaf ISIL raid in Syria"', *The Telegraph*, 9 August 2015, https://www.telegraph.co.uk/news/uknews/defence/11793011/SAS-took-part-in-Abu-Sayyaf-Isil-raid-in-Syria.html

11   Josie Ensor, 'US Special Forces carry out secret ground raid against ISIL in Syria, "killing at least 25 jihadists"', *The Telegraph*, 9 January 2017, https://www.telegraph.co.uk/news/2017/01/09/us-special-forces-carry-ground-raid-against-isil/

12   Brian Glyn Williams, *Counter Jihad: America's Military Experience in Afghanistan, Iraq and Syria* (Philadelphia, PA: University of Pennsylvania Press, 2017), p. 311.

13   Ibid., pp. 311–12.

14   Peter Baker, Helene Cooper, and David E. Sanger, 'Obama sends Special Operations Forces to help fight ISIS in Syria', *The New York Times*, 30 October 2015, https://www.nytimes.com/2015/10/31/world/obama-will-send-forces-to-syria-to-help-fight-the-islamic-state.html

15   Thomas Gibbons-Neff and Eric Schmitt, 'Pentagon considers using Special Operations Forces to continue missions in Syria', *The New York Times*, 21 December 2018, https://www.nytimes.com/2018/12/21/us/politics/pentagon-syria-iraq-kurds.html

16   BBC News, 'Two British soldiers injured in Islamic State attack in Syria', 6 January 2019, https://www.bbc.co.uk/news/uk-46772412

17   Australian Strategic Policy Institute (APSI), 'Strike from the Air: The First 100 Days of the Campaign Against ISIL' (December 2014), p. 38,

https://www.aspi.org.au/report/strike-air-first-100-days-campaign-against-isil

18  Tamir El-Ghobashy, Maria Abi-Habib, and Benoit Faucon, 'France directs kills of French fighters in ISIS', *Wall Street Journal*, 30 May 2017, https://www.wsj.com/articles/frances-special-forces-hunt-french-militants-fighting-for-islamic-state-1496090116

19  Ibid.

20  APSI, 'Strike from the Air', pp. 38–39.

21  Ibid., p. 40.

22  For more discussion on this distinction, see Andrew Mumford, *Proxy Warfare* (Cambridge: Polity, 2013), chapter 3.

23  Robinson, 'Assessment of the Politico-Military Campaign to Counter ISIL', pp. 50, 56.

24  Paul C. Hurley, Jr., Susan E. Henderson, and Sean J. Cannon, 'Considerations for Supporting a Train, Advise, and Assist Environment in Iraq', *Army Sustainment Magazine*, November 2016, https://alu.army.mil/alog/2016/NovDec16/PDF/176882.pdf

25  J. Patrick Work, 'Fighting the Islamic State By, With and Through', *Joint Forces Quarterly*, Vol. 89, No. 2 (2018), p. 56 (emphasis added).

26  Robinson, 'Assessment of the Politico-Military Campaign to Counter ISIL', pp. 51–53.

27  Eric Schmitt and Michael Gordon, 'US sees risks in assisting a compromised Iraqi force', *The New York Times*, 14 July 2014, https://www.nytimes.com/2014/07/14/world/middleeast/us-sees-risks-in-assisting-a-compromised-iraqi-force.html

28  Robinson, 'Assessment of the Politico-Military Campaign to Counter ISIL', p. 54.

29  Congressional Research Service (CRS), 'The "Islamic State" Crisis and US Policy', 12 November 2014, pp. 9–10, https://fas.org/sgp/crs/mideast/R43612.pdf

30  Andrew Tilghman, 'US advisory mission in Iraq remains limited in scope', *Military Times*, 20 October 2014, https://www.militarytimes.com/2014/10/20/u-s-advisory-mission-in-iraq-remains-limited-in-scope-and-impact/

31  APSI, 'Strike from the Air', p. 39.

32  CRS, 'The "Islamic State" Crisis and US Policy', p. 9.

33  Ibid., p. 9.

34  'OIR campaign reached turning point in Ramadi, commander says', Department of Defense press release, 10 August 2016, https://dod. defense.gov/News/Article/Article/910747/oir/

35  Global Coalition Against Daesh, 'Mission: Stabilising Liberated Areas', https://theglobalcoalition.org/en/mission/stabilising-liberated-areas/

36  'CJTF-OIR continues ISF training through multi-national efforts', Defense Visualization Information Distribution Service (DVIDS), 11 April 2019, https://www.dvidshub.net/news/317721/cjtf-oir-continues-isf-training-through-multi-national-efforts

37  Nicole Bauke, 'US, coalition form new advisory team to better train, assist Iraqi air force', *Air Force Times*, 5 February 2018, https://www. airforcetimes.com/flashpoints/2018/02/05/us-coalition-form-new-advisory-team-to-better-train-assist-iraqi-air-force/

38  Combined Joint Task Force – Operation Inherent Resolve (CJTF-OIR) press release, 'U.S. service members killed in Iraq', 9 March 2020, https:// www.inherentresolve.mil/Releases/News-Releases/Article/2105340/ us-service-members-killed-in-iraq/

39  A wonderful turn of phrase borrowed from the APSI report 'Strike from the Air', p. 7.

40  Eyal, Jonathan, and Elizabeth Quintana (eds.), 'Inherently Unresolved: The Military Operation Against ISIS', *RUSI Occasional Paper* (London: RUSI, 2015), https://rusi.org/publication/occasional-papers/inherently-unresolved-military-operation-against-isis

41  US Department of Defense, 'Operation Inherent Resolve' website, https://dod.defense.gov/OIR/

42  House of Commons Library briefing paper #8248, 'ISIS/Daesh: What Now for the Military Campaign in Iraq and Syria?', 7 March 2018, p. 10, https://researchbriefings.parliament.uk/ResearchBriefing/Summary/ CBP-8248#fullreport

43  Combined Joint Task Force – Operation Inherent Resolve (CJTF-OIR), 'Monthly Casualty Report', 27 September 2018, https://www. inherentresolve.mil/Media-Library/News-Releases/Article/1646397/

combined-joint-task-force-operation-inherent-resolve-monthly-civilian-casualty/

44　Richard Whittle, 'The unprecedented way America is fighting ISIS', *The New York Post*, 28 May 2016, https://nypost.com/2016/05/28/a-surreal-day-inside-our-war-against-isis/

45　Associated Press, 'US-led coalition: 1,257 civilians killed in airstrikes against ISIS', *Air Force Times*, 28 March 2019, https://www.airforcetimes.com/flashpoints/2019/03/29/us-led-coalition-1257-civilians-killed-in-airstrikes-against-isis/?utm_expid=.jFR93cgdTFyMrWXdYEtvgA.1&utm_referrer=https%3A%2F%2Fwww.google.com%2F#jwvideo

46　House of Commons Library, 'ISIS/Daesh', pp. 10, 15.

47　APSI, 'Strike from the Air', p. 8.

48　Kilcullen, *Blood Year*, p. 98.

49　Eyal and Quintana (eds.), 'Inherently Unresolved', p. 11.

50　Ibid., p. 12.

51　Robinson, 'Assessment of the Politico-Military Campaign to Counter ISIL', p. 44.

52　Oriana Pawlyk, 'ISIS kill missions: 1 in 5 drone flights includes a missile strike', *Air Force Times*, 30 March 2016, https://www.airforcetimes.com/news/your-air-force/2016/03/30/isis-kill-missions-1-in-5-drone-flights-includes-a-missile-strike/

53　Greg Miller, 'US launches secret drone campaign to hunt Islamic State leaders', *The Washington Post*, 1 September 2015, https://www.washingtonpost.com/world/national-security/us-launches-secret-drone-campaign-to-hunt-islamic-state-leaders-in-syria/2015/09/01/723b3e04-5033-11e5-933e-7d06c647a395_story.html

54　CJTF-OIR, 'Monthly Casualty Report', 27 September 2018.

55　Airwars, 'Limited Accountability: A Transparency Audit of the Coalition Air War Against So-Called Islamic State' (Oxford: Oxford Research Group, December 2016), https://airwars.org/report/limited-accountability-a-transparency-audit-of-the-coalition-air-war-against-so-called-islamic-state/

56　Azmat Khan and Anand Gopal, 'The uncounted', *The New York Times Magazine*, 16 November 2017, https://www.nytimes.com/

interactive/2017/11/16/magazine/uncounted-civilian-casualties-iraq-airstrikes.html

57 Quoted in BBC News, 'Military boss defends RAF bombings of IS', 8 June 2018, https://www.bbc.co.uk/news/uk-44404828

58 'General highlights airpower in fight against ISIS', Department of Defense news, 27 March 2018, https://dod.defense.gov/News/Article/Article/1477476/general-highlights-airpower-in-fight-against-isis/

59 House of Commons Library, 'ISIS/Daesh', p. 11.

60 Niall McCarthy, 'The cost of the air war against ISIS has reached $11 billion', *Forbes*, 1 February 2017, https://www.forbes.com/sites/niallmccarthy/2017/02/01/the-cost-of-the-air-war-against-isis-has-reached-11-billion-infographic/#33f8b2bcb120

## 5 Fighting ISIS by Other Means – The Cyber and Finance War

1 Associated Press, 'Obama vows not to relent against ISIS, "a bunch of killers with good social media"', *The Guardian*, 22 November 2015, https://www.theguardian.com/us-news/2015/nov/22/obama-addresses-isis-social-media-power

2 Colin P. Clarke, *After the Caliphate: The Islamic State and the Future of the Terrorist Diaspora* (Cambridge: Polity, 2019), pp. 65–66.

3 Imran Awan, 'Cyber-Extremism: ISIS and the Power of Social Media', *Social Science and Public Policy*, Vol. 54 (2017), p. 139.

4 J.M. Berger, 'How ISIS Games Twitter', *The Atlantic*, 16 June 2014, https://www.theatlantic.com/international/archive/2014/06/isis-iraq-twitter-social-media-strategy/372856/

5 BBC News, 'How ISIS is spreading its message online', 19 June 2014, https://www.bbc.co.uk/news/world-middle-east-27912569

6 Ibid.

7 James P. Farwell, 'The Media Strategy of ISIS', *Survival*, Vol. 56, No. 6 (2014), p. 51.

8    Mia Bloom, Hicham Tiflati, and John Horgan, 'Navigating ISIS's
     Preferred Platform: Telegram', *Terrorism and Political Violence*, Vol. 31,
     No. 6 (2019), pp. 1242–54.

9    David P. Fidler, "Terrorism, the Internet, and Islamic State's Defeat: It's
     Over But It's Not Over Yet', *Council on Foreign Relations blog* (28
     November 2017), https://www.cfr.org/blog/terrorism-internet-and-
     islamic-states-defeat-its-over-its-not-over

10   Andrew Byers and Tara Mooney, 'Winning the Cyber War Against ISIS',
     *Foreign Affairs*, 5 May 2017, https://www.foreignaffairs.com/articles/
     middle-east/2017-05-05/winning-cyberwar-against-isis

11   Ellen Nakashima, 'US military cyber operation to attack ISIS last year
     sparked heated debate over alerting allies', *The Washington Post*, 9 May
     2017, https://www.washingtonpost.com/world/national-security/
     us-military-cyber-operation-to-attack-isis-last-year-sparked-heated-
     debate-over-alerting-allies/2017/05/08/93a120a2-30d5-11e7-9dec-
     764dc781686f_story.html?utm_term=.ca1701f8708c

12   David E. Sanger, 'US cyberattacks target ISIS in a new line of
     combat', *The New York Times*, 24 April 2016, https://www.nytimes.
     com/2016/04/25/us/politics/us-directs-cyberweapons-at-isis-for-first-
     time.html

13   Dina Temple-Raston, 'How the US hacked ISIS', *NPR*, 26 September
     2019, https://www.npr.org/2019/09/26/763545811/how-the-u-s-
     hacked-isis

14   Ibid.

15   Dan Lamothe, 'How the Pentagon's cyber offensive against ISIS could
     shape the future for elite US forces', *The Washington Post*, 16 December
     2017, https://www.washingtonpost.com/news/checkpoint/wp/
     2017/12/16/how-the-pentagons-cyber-offensive-against-isis-could-
     shape-the-future-for-elite-u-s-forces/?utm_term=.0975443aa419

16   Quoted in Temple-Raston, 'How the US hacked ISIS'.

17   Global Coalition Against Daesh, 'Mission: Countering Daesh's
     Propaganda', https://theglobalcoalition.org/en/mission/countering-
     daeshs-propaganda/

18   Quoted in Temple-Raston, 'How the US hacked ISIS'.

19   Quoted in Sanger, 'US cyberattacks target ISIS in a new line of combat'.

20  Lamothe, 'How the Pentagon's cyber offensive against ISIS could shape the future for elite US forces'.

21  Jeppe Teglskov Jacobsen and Jens Ringsmose, 'Cyber-Bombing ISIS: Why Disclose What is Better Kept Secret?', *Global Affairs*, Vol. 3, No. 2 (2017), p. 126.

22  E.T. Brooking, 'Anonymous vs. the Islamic State', *Foreign Policy*, 13 November 2015, https://foreignpolicy.com/2015/11/13/anonymous-hackers-islamic-state-isis-chan-online-war/

23  Quoted in Brooking, 'Anonymous vs. the Islamic State'.

24  Mia Bloom and Chelsea Daymon, 'Assessing the Future Threat: ISIS's Virtual Caliphate', *Orbis*, Vol. 62, No. 3 (2018), pp. 372–88.

25  Tom Keatinge, 'The Importance of Financing in Enabling and Sustaining the Conflict in Syria (and Beyond)', *Perspectives on Terrorism*, Vol. 8, No. 4 (2014), p. 54.

26  Counter ISIS Finance Group, 'Leaders Joint Statement', 15 February 2018, https://home.treasury.gov/news/press-release/sm0294

27  US Treasury press release, 'Remarks of Acting Under-Secretary Adam Szubin on Countering the Financing of Terrorism at the Paul H. Nitze School of Advanced International Studies', 20 October 2016', https://www.treasury.gov/press-center/press-releases/Pages/jl0590.aspx

28  Matthew Levitt, 'Countering ISIL Financing: A Realistic Assessment', Washington Institute for Near East Policy briefing note (2 February 2015), https://www.washingtoninstitute.org/uploads/Documents/other/LevittStatement20150202-v3.pdf. Analysis by Hansen-Lewis and Shapiro in 2015 concluded that the total level of economic activity in ISIS-controlled territory was one-fifth of the rest of Iraq's and one-third of the rest of Syria's. See Jamie Hansen-Lewis and Jacob N. Shapiro, 'Understanding the Daesh Economy', *Perspectives on Terrorism*, Vol. 9, No. 4 (2015), p. 148.

29  Michael Jonsson, 'Funding the Islamic State: Sources of Revenue, Financing Requirements and Long-Term Vulnerabilities to Counter Measures', Swedish Defence Research Agency, Asia Security Briefing (December 2015), https://www.foi.se/download/18.7fd35d7f166c56ebe0bc0e8/1542369070574/Funding-the-Islamic-State_FOI-Memo-5525.pdf

30  Congressional Research Service (CRS), 'Islamic State Financing and US
    Policy Approaches' (R43980), 10 April 2015, p. 3, https://fas.org/sgp/crs/
    terror/R43980.pdf

31  Tom Keatinge, 'Defeating ISIS: How Financial Liabilities Will Undo the
    Jihadists', *RUSI Commentary blog* (27 October 2014), https://rusi.org/
    commentary/defeating-isis-how-financial-liabilities-will-undo-jihadists

32  CRS, 'Islamic State Financing and US Policy Approaches', pp. 9–10.

33  Loretta Napoleoni, *Merchants of Men: How Kidnapping, Ransom and
    Trafficking Fund Terrorism and ISIS* (London: Atlantic Books, 2018),
    p. 232.

34  Financial Action Task Force (FATF), 'Financing of the Terrorist
    Organisation Islamic State in Iraq and Levant (ISIL)', February 2015,
    p. 14, http://www.fatf-gafi.org/media/fatf/documents/reports/
    Financing-of-the-terrorist-organisation-ISIL.pdf

35  Mirren Gidda, 'Cash crunch in the Caliphate', *Newsweek*, 2 October
    2015, https://www.newsweek.com/2015/10/02/isis-are-facing-cash-
    crunch-caliphate-375490.html

36  Hansen-Lewis and Shapiro, 'Understanding the Daesh Economy',
    p. 149.

37  Jacob Shapiro, 'A Predictable Failure: The Political Economy of the
    Decline of the Islamic State', *CTC Sentinel*, Vol. 9, Issue 9 (September
    2016), p. 29, https://ctc.usma.edu/a-predictable-failure-the-political-
    economy-of-the-decline-of-the-islamic-state/

38  Yeganelu Torbati and Brett Wolf, 'In taking economic war to Islamic
    State, US developing new tools', *Reuters*, 24 November 2015, https://
    www.reuters.com/article/us-france-shooting-usa-sanctions-insight/
    in-taking-economic-war-to-islamic-state-u-s-developing-new-tools-id
    USKBN0TD0BJ20151124?feedType=RSS&feedName=worldNews

39  Joby Warrick, 'Inside the economic war against the Islamic State', *The
    Washington Post*, 31 December 2016, https://www.washingtonpost.com/
    world/national-security/take-them-back-to-the-19th-century-inside-
    the-economic-war-against-the-islamic-state/2016/12/30/5f91f514-ceb7-
    11e6-a747-d03044780a02_story.html

40  FATF, 'Financing of the Terrorist Organisation Islamic State in Iraq and
    the Levant (ISIL)', p. 5.

41  US Treasury press release, 'Remarks of Acting Under-Secretary Adam Szubin on Countering the Financing of Terrorism at the Paul H. Nitze School of Advanced International Studies'.

42  Ibid.

43  House of Commons Foreign Affairs Committee, 'The UK's Role in the Economic War Against ISIL', First Report of Session 2016-17 (HC 121), July 2016, p. 12, https://publications.parliament.uk/pa/cm201617/cmselect/cmfaff/121/121.pdf

44  NBC News, 'How to beat ISIS: blow up the money', 29 April 2016, https://www.nbcnews.com/storyline/isis-terror/how-beat-isis-blow-money-n564956

45  US Treasury press release, 'Remarks of Acting Under-Secretary Adam Szubin on Countering the Financing of Terrorism at the Paul H. Nitze School of Advanced International Studies'.

46  Torbati and Wolf, 'In taking economic war to Islamic State, US developing new tools'.

47  Nicholas Ryder, 'Out With the Old and ... In with the Old? A Critical Review of the Financial War on Terrorism on the Islamic State of Iraq and the Levant', *Studies in Conflict and Terrorism*, Vol. 41, No. 2 (2018), p. 81.

48  'Report of the Secretary-General on the threat posed by ISIL (Da'esh) to international peace and security and the range of United Nations efforts in support of Member States in countering the threat', United Nations Security Council, S/2016/92, 29 January 2016, pp. 18–19, https://www.un.org/sc/ctc/wp-content/uploads/2016/02/N1602353_EN.pdf

49  Ryder, 'Out With the Old and ... In with the Old?', pp. 87–89.

50  CRS, 'Islamic State Financing and US Policy Approaches', p. 11.

51  House of Commons Foreign Affairs Committee, 'The UK's Role in the Economic War Against ISIL', p. 14.

52  US Treasury press release, 'Remarks of Acting Under-Secretary Adam Szubin on Countering the Financing of Terrorism at the Paul H. Nitze School of Advanced International Studies'.

53  RAND Corporation, 'Financial Futures of the Islamic State of Iraq and the Levant' (Santa Monica, CA: RAND, 2017), p. 33, https://www.rand.org/pubs/conf_proceedings/CF361.html

54 Office of the Director of National Intelligence, 'ISIL Finances: Future Scenarios', 2016, https://www.dni.gov/files/PE/Documents/ISIL-Finances-Team-Intelligence.pdf

55 Torbati and Wolf, 'In taking economic war to Islamic State, US developing new tools'.

56 NBC News, 'How to beat ISIS: blow up the money'.

57 Joby Warrick, 'Retreating ISIS army smuggled a fortune in cash and gold out of Iraq and Syria', *The Washington Post*, 21 December 2018, https://www.washingtonpost.com/world/national-security/retreating-isis-army-smuggled-a-fortune-in-cash-and-gold-out-of-iraq-and-syria/2018/12/21/95087ffc-054b-11e9-9122-82e98f91ee6f_story.html

58 David Kenner, 'All ISIS has left is money: lots of it', *The Atlantic*, 24 March 2019, https://www.theatlantic.com/international/archive/2019/03/isis-caliphate-money-territory/584911/

## 6 The Alternative War: Russia, Iran, and Turkey Against ISIS

1 Lina Khatib and Lina Sinjab, 'Syria's Transactional State: How the Conflict Changed the Syrian State's Exercise of Power', Chatham House research paper (London: Chatham House, October 2018), pp. 21–22, https://www.chathamhouse.org/publication/syrias-transactional-state-how-conflict-changed-syrian-states-exercise-power

2 Seth Jones (ed.), 'Moscow's War in Syria' (Washington, DC: Center for Strategic and International Studies, May 2020), p. 1, https://www.csis.org/analysis/moscows-war-syria

3 Jonathan Steele, 'Putin in Syria', *London Review of Books*, 21 April 2016, https://www.lrb.co.uk/the-paper/v38/n08/jonathan-steele/putin-in-syria

4 David Kilcullen, *Blood Year: Islamic State and the Failures of the War on Terror* (London: Hurst, 2016), pp. 186–87.

5 Mark Mazzetti, Anne Barnard, and Eric Schmitt, 'Military success in Syria gives Putin upper hand in US proxy war', *The New York Times*,

6 August 2016, http://www.nytimes.com/2016/08/07/world/middleeast/military-syria-putin-us-proxy-war.html

6   Kilcullen, *Blood Year*, p. 188 (original emphasis).

7   Quoted in Mazzetti et al, 'Military success in Syria gives Putin upper hand'.

8   Liz Sly, 'Did US weapons supplied to Syrian rebels draw Russia into the conflict?', *The Washington Post*, 11 October 2015, https://www.washingtonpost.com/world/did-us-weapons-supplied-to-syrian-rebels-draw-russia-into-the-conflict/2015/10/11/268ce566-6dfc-11e5-91eb-27ad15c2b723_story.html

9   Christopher Phillips, *The Battle for Syria: International Rivalry in the New Middle East* (New Haven, CT: Yale University Press, 2016), p. 206.

10  Ibid., pp. 213–14.

11  Jones (ed.), 'Moscow's War in Syria', p. 2.

12  Shaun Walker, Kareem Shaheen, Martin Chulov, Spencer Ackerman, and Julian Borger, 'US accuses Russia of "throwing gasoline on the fire" of Syrian civil war', *The Guardian*, 1 October 2015, https://www.theguardian.com/world/2015/sep/30/russia-launches-first-airstrikes-against-targets-in-syria-says-us

13  Anne Barnard and Thomas Erdbrink, 'ISIS makes gains in Syria territory bombed by Russia', *The New York Times*, 9 October 2015, https://www.nytimes.com/2015/10/10/world/middleeast/hussein-hamedani-iran-general-killed-in-syria.html

14  Emil Aslan Souleimanov and Katrina Petrtylova, 'Russia's Policy Toward the Islamic State', *Middle East Policy*, Vol. 22, No. 3 (2015), p. 68, https://mepc.org/russias-policy-toward-islamic-state

15  Phillips, *The Battle for Syria*, p. 206.

16  Igor Sutyagin, 'Russia', in Jonathan Eyal and Elizabeth Quintana (eds.), 'Inherently Unresolved: The Military Operation Against ISIS', *RUSI Occasional Paper* (London: RUSI, 2015), p. 42, https://rusi.org/sites/default/files/countering-isis-regional-implications.pdf

17  Bettina Renz, *Russia's Military Revival* (Cambridge: Polity, 2018), p. 2.

18  Keith Johnson, 'Putin's Mediterranean Power Play in Syria', *Foreign Policy*, 2 October 2015, https://foreignpolicy.com/2015/10/02/putins-mediterranean-power-play-in-syria-navy-tartus-fleet/

19  Jones (ed.), 'Moscow's War in Syria', p. 1.

20  Associated Press, 'Russia says tens of thousands of its troops fought in Syria', 22 August 2018, https://www.apnews.com/ f787223e4fee4946be853662505e95c4

21  Jones (ed.), 'Moscow's War in Syria', p. 1.

22  Ali M. Ansari, 'Iran', in Jonathan Eyal and Elizabeth Quintana (eds.), 'Inherently Unresolved: The Military Operation Against ISIS', *RUSI Occasional Paper* (London: RUSI, 2015), p. 31, https://rusi.org/sites/ default/files/countering-isis-regional-implications.pdf

23  Soufan Center, 'Iran's Playbook: Deconstructing Tehran's Regional Strategy' (Washington, DC, May 2019), p. 14, https://thesoufancenter. org/research/irans-playbook-deconstructing-tehrans-regional-strategy/

24  Ibid., p. 15.

25  Ansari, 'Iran', p. 34.

26  Soufan Center, 'Iran's Playbook', p. 6.

27  Dina Esfandiary and Ariane Tabatabai, 'Iran's ISIS Policy', *International Affairs*, Vol. 91, No. 1 (2015), p. 2.

28  Ibid., p. 9.

29  Ibid., p. 7

30  Hugh Naylor, 'Iranian media is revealing that scores of the country's fighters are dying in Syria', *The Washington Post*, 27 November 2015, https://www.washingtonpost.com/world/iranian-media-is-revealing- that-scores-of-the-countrys-fighters-are-dying-in-syria/2015/11/27/ 294deb02-8ca0-11e5-934c-a369c80822c2_story.html

31  Esfandiary and Tabatabai, 'Iran's ISIS Policy', p. 7.

32  International Crisis Group, 'Arming Iraq's Kurds: Fighting IS, Inviting Conflict', *Middle East Report*, No. 158 (12 May 2015), pp. 12–13, https:// www.crisisgroup.org/middle-east-north-africa/gulf-and-arabian- peninsula/iraq/arming-iraq-s-kurds-fighting-inviting-conflict

33  Quoted in Ibid., p.13.

34  Michael Weiss and Hassan Hassan, *ISIS: Inside the Army of Terror* (New York: Regan Arts, 2015), pp. 137–38.

35  Kilcullen, *Blood Year*, p. 138.

36  Ibid., p. 138.

37  Ibid., p. 159.

38 Hassan Hassan, 'Iran won't surrender militias that conduct Assad's war', *The National*, 10 January 2016, http://www.thenational.ae/opinion/comment/iran-wont-surrender-militias-that-conduct-assads-war

39 Martin Chulov, 'Amid the bloody chaos of Syria, Iran's game plan is laid bare: a path to the sea', *The Observer*, 9 October 2016, https://www.theguardian.com/world/2016/oct/08/iran-iraq-syria-isis-land-corridor

40 Dexter Filkins, 'The dangers posed by the killing of Qassem Suleimani', *The New Yorker*, 3 January 2020, https://www.newyorker.com/news/daily-comment/the-dangers-posed-by-the-killing-of-qassem-suleimani

41 Brian Bender, 'Pentagon halts fight against ISIS in Iraq amid new threats to bases', *Politico*, 5 January 2020, https://www.politico.com/news/2020/01/05/pentagon-halts-fight-isis-iraq-bases-094140

42 Dan Sabbagh, 'Anti-ISIS coalition suspends operations as Iraqi MPs vote to expel US troops', *The Guardian*, 5 January 2020, https://www.theguardian.com/world/2020/jan/05/anti-isis-coalition-suspends-operations-as-iraqi-mps-vote-to-expel-us-troops

43 Helene Cooper and Alissa J. Rubin, 'The US seemed to be leaving Iraq but it was all an 'honest mistake'', *New York Times*, 6 January 2020, https://www.nytimes.com/2020/01/06/world/middleeast/iran-letter-withdrawal-iraq.html

44 Jay Solomon and Carol E. Lee, 'Iran's Ayatollah sends new letter to Obama amid nuclear talks', *The Wall Street Journal*, 13 February 2015, https://www.wsj.com/articles/irans-ayatollah-sends-new-letter-to-obama-amid-nuclear-talks-1423872638

45 BBC News, 'US to expel last Iranian boot from Syria – Pompeo', 10 January 2019, https://www.bbc.co.uk/news/world-middle-east-46828810

46 Ash Carter, 'A Lasting Defeat: The Campaign to Destroy ISIS', Belfer Center special report (October 2017), p. 39, https://www.belfercenter.org/LastingDefeat

47 Phillips, *The Battle for Syria*, pp. 210–11.

48 William Harris, *Quicksilver War: Syria, Iraq and the Spiral of Conflict* (London: Hurst, 2018), p. 143.

49 Ibid., p. 144.

50  Constanze Letsch, 'Turkey denies new deal reached to open airbases to US in fight against ISIS', *The Guardian*, 13 October 2014, https://www.theguardian.com/world/2014/oct/13/turkey-denies-agreement-open-air-bases-us-isis

51  Harris, *Quicksilver War*, p. 146.

52  Ibid., p. 146.

53  Kareem Shaheen, Shaun Walker, Julian Borger, and David Smith, 'Putin condemns Turkey after Russian warplane downed near Syria border', *The Guardian*, 24 November 2015, https://www.theguardian.com/world/2015/nov/24/turkey-shoots-down-jet-near-border-with-syria

54  Louisa Loveluck, 'Turkish president threatens to "drown" US-backed force in Syria', *The Washington Post*, 15 January 2018, https://www.washingtonpost.com/world/turkish-president-threatens-todrown-us-backed-force-in-syria/2018/01/15/e7789850-f9e7-11e7-b832-8c26844b74fb_story.html

55  Mert Ozkan and Ellen Francis, 'Airstrikes pound Syria's Afrin as Turkey launches "Operation Olive Branch"', *Reuters*, 20 January 2018, https://uk.reuters.com/article/uk-mideast-crisis-syria-turkey/airstrikes-pound-syrias-afrin-as-turkey-launches-operation-olive-branch-idUKKBN1F90RS

56  Can Kasapoglu and Sinan Ulgen, 'Operation Olive Branch: A Political-Military Assessment', Centre for Economics and Foreign Policy Studies (EDAM) occasional paper (January 2018), p. 1, https://edam.org.tr/en/operation-olive-branch-a-political-military-assessment/

57  Mevlut Çavuşoğlu, 'The Meaning of Operation Olive Branch', *Foreign Policy*, 5 April 2018, https://foreignpolicy.com/2018/04/05/the-meaning-of-operation-olive-branch/

58  Reuters, 'Exclusive: US commanders recommend letting Kurdish fighters in Syria keep weapons', 28 December 2018, https://uk.reuters.com/article/uk-mideast-crisis-syria-usa-exclusive/exclusive-u-s-commanders-recommend-letting-kurdish-fighters-in-syria-keep-weapons-idUKKCN1OR1OH

59  Patrick Wintour, 'Putin brings Iran and Turkey together in bold Syria peace plan', *The Guardian*, 22 November 2017, https://www.theguardian.

com/world/2017/nov/22/iranian-and-turkish-leaders-arrive-in-russia-for-syria-talks-with-putin

60  Khatib and Sinjab, 'Syria's Transactional State', p. 23.

61  Sam Heller, 'Russia is in Charge in Syria: How Moscow Took Control of the Battlefield and Negotiating Table', *War on the Rocks*, 28 June 2016, https://warontherocks.com/2016/06/russia-is-in-charge-in-syria-how-moscow-took-control-of-the-battlefield-and-negotiating-table/

62  Vladimir Putin, 'Speech at UN General Assembly', 28 September 2015, reprinted in *Washington Post*, 'Read Putin's UN General Assembly Speech', https://www.washingtonpost.com/news/worldviews/wp/2015/09/28/read-putins-u-n-general-assembly-speech/

63  Paul McLeary, 'Russia winning info & electronic war in Syria, US and UK generals warn', *Breaking Defense*, 9 October 2018, https://breakingdefense.com/2018/10/russia-winning-information-electronic-war-over-syria-us-uk-generals-warn/

# Conclusion

1   Jason Burke, 'Rise and fall of ISIS: its dream of a caliphate is over, so what now?', *The Guardian*, 21 October 2017, https://www.theguardian.com/world/2017/oct/21/isis-caliphate-islamic-state-raqqa-iraq-islamist

2   'Ground offensive begins for Operation Roundup, phase three', CJTF-OIR press release, 11 September 2018, https://www.centcom.mil/MEDIA/NEWS-ARTICLES/News-Article-View/Article/1626665/ground-offensive-begins-for-operation-roundup-phase-three/

3   Dylan Malyasov, 'French military announces start of Iraq withdrawal', *Defence Blog*, 7 April 2019, https://defence-blog.com/army/french-military-announces-start-of-iraq-withdrawal.html

4   'Statement by Ministers of the Global Coalition to Defeat ISIS/Daesh', US State Department press release, 6 February 2019, https://sy.usembassy.gov/statement-by-ministers-of-the-global-coalition-to-defeat-isis-daesh/

5   Colin P. Clarke, *After the Caliphate: The Islamic State and the Future of the Terrorist Diaspora* (Cambridge: Polity, 2019), pp. 2, 9.

6    Maher Chmaytelli and Ahmed Aboulenein, 'Iraq declares final victory over Islamic State', *Reuters*, 9 December 2017, https://www.reuters.com/article/us-mideast-crisis-iraq-islamicstate/iraq-declares-final-victory-over-islamic-state-idUSKBN1E30B9

7    Josh Rogin, 'Trump undermines his entire national security team on Syria', *The Washington Post*, 19 December 2018, https://www.washingtonpost.com/opinions/2018/12/19/trump-undermines-his-entire-national-security-team-syria/

8    Quoted in David E. Sanger and Julian E. Barnes, 'On North Korea and Iran, intelligence chiefs contradict Trump', *The New York Times*, 29 January 2019, https://www.nytimes.com/2019/01/29/us/politics/kim-jong-trump.html

9    John R. Allen, 'I was special envoy to fight the Islamic State: Our gains are now at risk', *The Washington Post*, 3 January 2019, https://www.washingtonpost.com/opinions/i-was-special-envoy-to-fight-the-islamic-state-trump-could-unravel-our-gains/2019/01/03/2339f1a4-0ebe-11e9-84fc-d58c33d6c8c7_story.html

10   Robin Wright, 'The ignominious end of the ISIS caliphate', *The New Yorker*, 17 October 2017, https://www.newyorker.com/news/news-desk/the-ignominious-end-of-the-isis-caliphate

11   Ben Taub, 'Iraq's post-ISIS campaign of revenge', *The New Yorker*, December 2018, https://www.newyorker.com/magazine/2018/12/24/iraqs-post-isis-campaign-of-revenge

12   Liesbeth van der Heide, Charlie Winter, and Shiraz Maher, 'The Cost of Crying Victory: Policy Implications of the Islamic State's Territorial Collapse' (The Hague: International Centre for Counter-Terrorism report, November 2018), p. 4, https://icct.nl/publication/the-cost-of-crying-victory-policy-implications-of-the-islamic-states-territorial-collapse/

13   National Co-ordinator for Security and Counter-Terrorism (Dutch Ministry of Justice and Security), 'A Perspective on the Transformation of ISIS Following the Fall of the 'Caliphate', The Hague, Winter 2018, p. 55, https://english.nctv.nl/binaries/WEB_112216_ENG%20Rapport%20Transformatie_tcm

14   Global Coalition Against Daesh, 'Statement', 23 March 2020, https://theglobalcoalition.org/en/statement-on-behalf-of-the-global-coalition-to-defeat-daesh-isis/

15 Robin Wright, 'The breathtaking unravelling of the Middle East after Qassem Suleimani's death', *The New Yorker*, 6 January 2020, https://www.newyorker.com/news/our-columnists/the-breathtaking-unravelling-of-the-middle-east-after-suleimanis-death

16 Truls Hallberg Tønnesen, , 'The Islamic State After the Caliphate', *Perspectives on Terrorism*, Vol. 13, No. 1 (2019), p. 1.

17 International Crisis Group, 'Contending with ISIS in the Time of Coronavirus' (31 March 2020), https://www.crisisgroup.org/global/contending-isis-time-coronavirus

18 Combined Joint Task Force – Operation Inherent Resolve (CJTF-OIR), 'Statement on the repositioning of forces', 20 March 2020, https://www.inherentresolve.mil/Releases/News-Releases/Article/2119563/cjtf-oir-statement-on-repositioning-of-forces/#:~:text=%E2%80%9CThe%20Coalition%20is%20adjusting%20its,force%20during%20the%20Coronavirus%20pandemic

19 Michael Knight, 'How the Islamic State feeds on coronavirus', *Politico*, 8 April 2020, https://www.politico.com/news/magazine/2020/04/08/how-the-islamic-state-feeds-on-coronavirus-175192

20 UK Ministry of Defence press release, 'UK personnel to drawdown from Iraq', 19 March 2020, https://www.gov.uk/government/news/uk-personnel-to-drawdown-from-iraq

21 Chad Garland, 'US special operations troops turn to drones to remotely advise Iraqis', Stars and Stripes, 4 May 2020, https://www.stripes.com/news/middle-east/us-special-operations-troops-turn-to-drones-to-remotely-advise-iraqis-1.628337

22 Knight, 'How the Islamic State feeds on coronavirus'.

23 Ibid.

24 BBC News, 'Abu Bakr al-Baghdadi: what his death means for IS in Syria', 27 October 2019, https://www.bbc.co.uk/news/world-middle-east-50199437

25 *The Economist*, 'Decapitated, not defeated', 2 November 2019, https://www.economist.com/middle-east-and-africa/2019/11/02/islamic-state-after-the-death-of-abu-bakr-al-baghdadi

26 Martin Chulov and Mohammed Rasool, 'Isis founding member confirmed by spies as group's new leader', *The Guardian*, 20 January

2020, https://www.theguardian.com/world/2020/jan/20/isis-leader-
confirmed-amir-mohammed-abdul-rahman-al-mawli-al-salbi

27   Clarke, *After the Caliphate*, p. 3.

28   BBC News, 'US-backed Syrian fighters "overrun IS encampment"', 19
     March 2019, https://www.bbc.co.uk/news/world-middle-east-47628209

29   Clarke, *After the Caliphate*, p. 41.

30   Hassan Hassan, "Insurgents Again: The Islamic State's Calculated
     Reversion to Attrition in the Syria–Iraq Border Region and Beyond',
     *CTC Sentinel*, Vol. 10, Issue 11 (December 2017), pp. 1–8, https://ctc.
     usma.edu/insurgents-again-the-islamic-states-calculated-reversion-to-
     attrition-in-the-syria-iraq-border-region-and-beyond/

31   Mike Giglio, *Shatter the Nations: ISIS and the War for the Caliphate*
     (New York: Public Affairs, 2019), p. 274.

32   Colin P. Clarke, 'The Post-Caliphate Caliph', *Foreign Policy*, 29 April
     2019, https://foreignpolicy.com/2019/04/29/the-post-caliphate-caliph/

33   Aziz Ahmad, 'Undefeated, ISIS is back in Iraq', *The New York Review of
     Books blog*, 13 February 2019, https://www.nybooks.com/
     daily/2019/02/13/undefeated-isis-is-back-in-iraq/

34   For a thorough discussion of these options, see National Co-ordinator
     for Security and Counter-Terrorism (Dutch Ministry of Justice and
     Security), 'A Perspective on the Transformation of ISIS Following the
     Fall of the "Caliphate"', The Hague, Winter 2018.

35   Tom Stevenson, 'How to run a Caliphate', *London Review of Books*,
     20 June 2019, https://www.lrb.co.uk/the-paper/v41/n12/tom-stevenson/
     how-to-run-a-caliphate

36   Giglio, *Shatter the Nations*, p. 3.

37   Thomas Gibbons-Neff, 'The American intervention against ISIS is just
     another chapter in an endless war', *The New York Times Magazine*,
     29 March 2019, https://www.nytimes.com/2019/03/29/magazine/
     isis-syria-defeat.html

38   Jonathan Eyal and Elizabeth Quintana (eds.), 'Inherently Unresolved:
     The Military Operation Against ISIS', *RUSI Occasional Paper* (London:
     RUSI, 2015), p. 1, https://rusi.org/publication/occasional-papers/
     inherently-unresolved-military-operation-against-isis

39   Ibid, p. 1.

40  Congressional Research Service (CRS), 'Coalition Contributions to Countering the Islamic State', 24 August 2016, p. 6, https://fas.org/sgp/crs/natsec/R44135.pdf

41  Kenneth M. Pollack, 'Iraq Situation Report, Part I: The Military Campaign Against ISIS' (Washington, DC: Brookings Institute, 28 March 2016), https://www.brookings.edu/blog/markaz/2016/03/28/iraq-situation-report-part-i-the-military-campaign-against-isis/

42  C. Alexander Ohlers, 'Operation Inherent Resolve and the Islamic State: Assessing "Aggressive Containment"', *Orbis*, Vol. 61, No. 2 (2017), p. 201.

# Bibliography

## Primary sources

'CJTF-OIR continues ISF training through multi-national efforts', Defense Visualization Information Distribution Service (DVIDS), 11 April 2019, https://www.dvidshub.net/news/317721/cjtf-oir-continues-isf-training-through-multi-national-efforts

'Coalition announces shift in focus as Iraq campaign progresses', Combined Joint Task Force Operation Inherent Resolve news release, 5 February 2018, https://dod.defense.gov/News/Article/Article/1432692/coalition-announces-shift-in-focus-as-iraq-campaign-progresses/

Congressional Research Service (CRS), 'The "Islamic State" Crisis and US Policy', 12 November 2014, https://fas.org/sgp/crs/mideast/R43612.pdf

Congressional Research Service (CRS), 'Islamic State Financing and US Policy Approaches' (R43980), 10 April 2015, https://fas.org/sgp/crs/terror/R43980.pdf

Congressional Research Service (CRS), 'Coalition Contributions to Countering the Islamic State', 24 August 2016, https://fas.org/sgp/crs/natsec/R44135.pdf

Combined Joint Task Force – Operation Inherent Resolve (CJTF-OIR) website, 'Campaign Design', https://www.inherentresolve.mil/campaign/

Combined Joint Task Force – Operation Inherent Resolve (CJTF-OIR), 'Monthly Casualty Report', 27 September 2018, https://www.inherentresolve.mil/Media-Library/News-Releases/Article/1646397/combined-joint-task-force-operation-inherent-resolve-monthly-civilian-casualty/

Combined Joint Task Force – Operation Inherent Resolve (CJTF-OIR) press release, 'U.S. service members killed in Iraq', 9 March 2020, https://www.inherentresolve.mil/Releases/News-Releases/Article/2105340/us-service-members-killed-in-iraq/

Combined Joint Task Force – Operation Inherent Resolve (CJTF-OIR), 'Statement on the repositioning of forces', 20 March 2020, https://www.inherentresolve.mil/Releases/News-Releases/Article/2119563/cjtf-oir-

statement-on-repositioning-of-forces/#:~:text=%E2%80%9CThe%20
Coalition%20is%20adjusting%20its,force%20during%20the%20
Coronavirus%20pandemic

Counter ISIS Finance Group, 'Leaders Joint Statement', 15 February 2018,
https://home.treasury.gov/news/press-release/sm0294

Department of Defense press release, '1 year in: officials assess anti-ISIL
progress', 6 August 2015, https://www.defense.gov/Explore/News/Article/
Article/612754/1-year-in-officials-assess-anti-isil-progress/

Financial Action Task Force (FATF), 'Financing of the Terrorist
Organisation Islamic State in Iraq and Levant (ISIL)', February 2015,
http://www.fatf-gafi.org/media/fatf/documents/reports/Financing-of-
the-terrorist-organisation-ISIL.pdf

'General highlights airpower in fight against ISIS', Department of Defense
news, 27 March 2018, https://dod.defense.gov/News/Article/
Article/1477476/general-highlights-airpower-in-fight-against-isis/

Global Coalition Against Daesh, 'Mission: Countering Daesh's Propaganda',
https://theglobalcoalition.org/en/mission/countering-daeshs-propaganda/

Global Coalition Against Daesh, 'Mission: Stabilising Liberated Areas',
https://theglobalcoalition.org/en/mission/stabilising-liberated-areas/

Global Coalition Against Daesh, 'Statement', 23 March 2020, https://
theglobalcoalition.org/en/statement-on-behalf-of-the-global-coalition-
to-defeat-daesh-isis/

'Ground offensive begins for Operation Roundup, phase three', CJTF-OIR
press release, 11 September 2018, https://www.centcom.mil/MEDIA/
NEWS-ARTICLES/News-Article-View/Article/1626665/ground-
offensive-begins-for-operation-roundup-phase-three/

House Joint Resolution 124, Continuing Appropriations Resolution #2,015,
113th Congress (2013–14), https://www.congress.gov/bill/113th-
congress/house-joint-resolution/124

House of Commons Foreign Affairs Committee, 'The UK's Role in the
Economic War Against ISIL', First Report of Session 2016-17 (HC 121),
July 2016, https://publications.parliament.uk/pa/cm201617/cmselect/
cmfaff/121/121.pdf

House of Commons Library briefing paper #8248, 'ISIS/Daesh: What Now
for the Military Campaign in Iraq and Syria?', 7 March 2018, https://

researchbriefings.parliament.uk/ResearchBriefing/Summary/CBP-8248#fullreport

Inaugural Address of President Donald J. Trump, 20 January 2017, https://www.whitehouse.gov/inaugural-address

'Kerry, Hagel Joint Statement on ISIL Meeting with Key Partners', US Embassy in Syria press release, 5 September 2014, https://sy.usembassy.gov/kerry-hagel-joint-statement-isil-meeting-key-partners/

'Letter to D-ISIS Coalition Partners on the Progress of the Past Year', Brett McGurk, Special Presidential Envoy for the Global Coalition to Counter ISIS, 29 December 2017, https://www.state.gov/s/seci/2017remarks/276806.htm

National Co-ordinator for Security and Counter-Terrorism (Dutch Ministry of Justice and Security), 'A Perspective on the Transformation of ISIS Following the Fall of the "Caliphate"', The Hague, Winter 2018.

Office of the Director of National Intelligence, 'ISIL Finances: Future Scenarios', 2016, https://www.dni.gov/files/PE/Documents/ISIL-Finances-Team-Intelligence.pdf

'OIR campaign reached turning point in Ramadi, commander says', Department of Defense press release, 10 August 2016, https://dod.defense.gov/News/Article/Article/910747/oir/

Presidential Memorandum, 'Plan to Defeat the Islamic State of Iraq and Syria', 28 January 2017, https://www.whitehouse.gov/presidential-actions/presidential-memorandum-plan-defeat-islamic-state-iraq-syria/

Putin, Vladimir, 'Speech at UN General Assembly', 28 September 2015, reprinted in *Washington Post*, 'Read Putin's UN General Assembly Speech', https://www.washingtonpost.com/news/worldviews/wp/2015/09/28/read-putins-u-n-general-assembly-speech/

Remarks of President Obama and President Ilves of Estonia in Joint Press Conference, 3 September 2014, https://obamawhitehouse.archives.gov/the-press-office/2014/09/03/remarks-president-obama-and-president-ilves-estonia-joint-press-confer-0

'Report of the Secretary-General on the threat posed by ISIL (Da'esh) to international peace and security and the range of United Nations efforts in support of Member States in countering the threat', United Nations

Security Council, S/2016/92, 29 January 2016, https://www.un.org/sc/ctc/wp-content/uploads/2016/02/N1602353_EN.pdf

'Statement by the President', White House, 7 August 2014, https://obamawhitehouse.archives.gov/the-press-office/2014/08/07/statement-president

'Statement by the President on ISIL', White House, 10 September 2014, https://obamawhitehouse.archives.gov/the-press-office/2014/09/10/statement-president-isil-1

'Statement by Ministers of the Global Coalition to Defeat ISIS/Daesh', US State Department press release, 6 February 2019, https://sy.usembassy.gov/statement-by-ministers-of-the-global-coalition-to-defeat-isis-daesh/

UK Ministry of Defence press release, 'UK provides further equipment to Kurdish fighters tackling ISIL', 22 June 2015, https://www.gov.uk/government/news/uk-provides-further-equipment-to-kurdish-fighters-tackling-isil

UK Ministry of Defence press release, 'UK personnel to drawdown from Iraq', 19 March 2020, https://www.gov.uk/government/news/uk-personnel-to-drawdown-from-iraq

US Department of Defense, 'Operation Inherent Resolve' website, https://dod.defense.gov/OIR/

US Department of State, 'Joint Statement issued by partners at the Counter-ISIL Coalition Ministerial Meeting', 3 December 2014, https://2009-2017.state.gov/r/pa/prs/ps/2014/12/234627.htm

US National Security Strategy, Washington, DC, December 2017, https://www.whitehouse.gov/wp-content/uploads/2017/12/NSS-Final-12-18-2017-0905.pdf

US Treasury press release, 'Remarks of Acting Under-Secretary Adam Szubin on Countering the Financing of Terrorism at the Paul H. Nitze School of Advanced International Studies', 20 October 2016', https://www.treasury.gov/press-center/press-releases/Pages/jl0590.aspx

## Secondary sources

Al-Dayel, Nadia, Andrew Mumford, and Kevin Bales, '"Not Yet Dead": The Establishment and Regulation of Slavery by the Islamic State', *Studies in*

*Conflict and Terrorism*, https://www.tandfonline.com/doi/full/10.1080/1 057610X.2020.1711590

Al-Istrabadi, Feisal, and Sumit Ganguly (eds.), *The Future of ISIS: Regional and International Implications* (Washington, DC: Brookings Institution Press, 2018).

Allawi, Ali A., *The Occupation of Iraq: Winning the War, Losing the Peace* (New Haven, CT: Yale University Press, 2007).

Auerswald, David P., and Stephen M. Saideman, *NATO in Afghanistan: Fighting Together, Fighting Alone* (Princeton, NJ: Princeton University Press, 2014).

Awan, Imran, 'Cyber-Extremism: ISIS and the Power of Social Media', *Social Science and Public Policy*, Vol. 54 (2017), pp. 138–49.

Bloom, Mia, and Chelsea Daymon, 'Assessing the Future Threat: ISIS's Virtual Caliphate', *Orbis*, Vol. 62, No. 3 (2018), pp. 372–88.

Bloom, Mia, Hicham Tiflati, and John Horgan, 'Navigating ISIS's Preferred Platform: Telegram', *Terrorism and Political Violence*, Vol. 31, No. 6 (2019), pp. 1242–54.

Brooking, E.T., 'Anonymous vs. the Islamic State', *Foreign Policy*, 13 November 2015, https://foreignpolicy.com/2015/11/13/anonymous-hackers-islamic-state-isis-chan-online-war/

Byers, Andrew, and Tara Mooney, 'Winning the Cyber War Against ISIS', *Foreign Affairs*, 5 May 2017, https://www.foreignaffairs.com/articles/middle-east/2017-05-05/winning-cyberwar-against-isis

Byman, Daniel, 'ISIS Goes Global', *Foreign Affairs*, Vol. 95, No. 2 (2016), pp. 76–85.

Byman, Daniel, 'Understanding the Islamic State: A Review Essay', *International Security*, Vol. 40, No. 4 (2016), pp. 127–65.

Byman, Daniel, and Ian A. Merritt, 'The New American Way of War: Special Operations Forces in the War on Terrorism', *Washington Quarterly*, Vol. 41, No. 2 (2018), pp. 79–93.

Carson, Austin, and Michael Poznansky, 'The Logic for (Shoddy) US Covert Action in Syria', *War on the Rocks*, 21 July 2016, https://warontherocks.com/2016/07/the-logic-for-shoddy-u-s-covert-action-in-syria/

Çavuşoğlu, Mevlut, 'The Meaning of Operation Olive Branch', *Foreign Policy*, 5 April 2018, https://foreignpolicy.com/2018/04/05/the-meaning-of-operation-olive-branch/

Chandrasekaran, Rajiv, *Little America: The War within the War for Afghanistan* (London: Bloomsbury, 2013).

Clarke, Colin P., *After the Caliphate: The Islamic State and the Future of the Terrorist Diaspora* (Cambridge: Polity, 2019).

Clarke, Colin P., 'The Post-Caliphate Caliph', *Foreign Policy*, 29 April 2019, https://foreignpolicy.com/2019/04/29/the-post-caliphate-caliph/

Cockburn, Patrick, *The Rise of Islamic State: ISIS and the New Sunni Revolution* (London: Verso, 2015).

Doeser, Fredrik, 'Historical Experiences, Strategic Culture, and Strategic Behaviour: Poland in the Anti-ISIS Coalition', *Defence Studies*, Vol. 18, No. 4 (2018), pp. 454–73.

Doeser, Fredrik, and Joackim Eidenfalk, 'Using Strategic Culture to Understand Participation in Expeditionary Operations: Australia, Poland, and the Coalition Against the Islamic State', *Contemporary Security Policy*, Vol. 40, No. 1 (2019), pp. 4–29.

English, Richard, 'The ISIS Crisis', *Journal of Terrorism Research*, Vol. 8, No. 1 (2017), pp. 90–94.

Esfandiary, Dina, and Ariane Tabatabai, 'Iran's ISIS Policy', *International Affairs*, Vol. 91, No. 1 (2015), pp. 1–15.

Eyal, Jonathan, and Elizabeth Quintana (eds.), 'Inherently Unresolved: Regional Politics and the Counter-ISIS Campaign', *RUSI Occasional Paper* (London: RUSI, 2015), https://rusi.org/sites/default/files/countering-isis-regional-implications.pdf

Farrell, Theo, *Unwinnable: Britain's War in Afghanistan, 2001–2014* (London: Bodley Head, 2017).

Farwell, James P., 'The Media Strategy of ISIS', *Survival*, Vol. 56, No. 6 (2014), pp. 49–55.

Ferenzi, Steve, 'Beyond Half Measures: Influencing Syria's Political Order through Non-state Proxies', *Small Wars Journal*, May 2016, https://smallwarsjournal.com/jrnl/art/beyond-half-measures-influencing-syria's-political-order-through-non-state-proxies

Fishman, Ben, 'Defining ISIS', *Survival*, Vol. 58, No. 1 (2016), pp. 179–88.

Fromson, James, and Steven Simon, 'ISIS: The Dubious Paradise of Apocalypse Now', *Survival*, Vol. 57, No. 3 (2015), pp. 7–56.

Giglio, Mike, *Shatter the Nations: ISIS and the War for the Caliphate* (New York: Public Affairs, 2019).

Gill, Paul, *Lone Actor Terrorists: A Behavioural Analysis* (Abingdon: Routledge, 2016).

Gordon, Michael, and Bernard Trainor, *Cobra II: The Inside Story of the Invasion and Occupation of Iraq* (London: Atlantic Books, 2006).

Groh, Tyrone L., *Proxy War: The Least Bad Option* (Stanford, CA: Stanford University Press, 2019).

Haesebrouck, Tim, 'Democratic Participation in the Air Strikes Against Islamic State: A Qualitative Comparative Analysis', *Foreign Policy Analysis*, Vol. 14, No. 2 (2018), pp. 254–75.

Hansen-Lewis, Jamie, and Jacob N. Shapiro, 'Understanding the Daesh Economy', *Perspectives on Terrorism*, Vol. 9, No. 4 (2015), pp. 142–55.

Harris, William, *Quicksilver War: Syria, Iraq and the Spiral of Conflict* (London: Hurst, 2018).

Hashim, Ahmed S., *Insurgency and Counter-Insurgency in Iraq* (London: Hurst, 2006).

Hassan, Hassan, 'Insurgents Again: The Islamic State's Calculated Reversion to Attrition in the Syria–Iraq Border Region and Beyond', *CTC Sentinel*, Vol. 10, Issue 11 (December 2017), https://ctc.usma.edu/insurgents-again-the-islamic-states-calculated-reversion-to-attrition-in-the-syria-iraq-border-region-and-beyond/

Heller, Sam, 'Russia is in Charge in Syria: How Moscow Took Control of the Battlefield and Negotiating Table', *War on the Rocks*, 28 June 2016, https://warontherocks.com/2016/06/russia-is-in-charge-in-syria-how-moscow-took-control-of-the-battlefield-and-negotiating-table/

Hughes, Geraint Alun, 'Syria and the Perils of Proxy Warfare', *Small Wars and Insurgencies*, Vol. 25, No. 3 (2014), pp. 522–38.

Hurley, Jr., Paul C., Susan E. Henderson, and Sean J. Cannon, 'Considerations for Supporting a Train, Advise, and Assist Environment in Iraq', *Army Sustainment Magazine*, November 2016, https://alu.army.mil/alog/2016/NovDec16/PDF/176882.pdf

Jacobsen, Jeppe Teglskov, and Jens Ringsmose, 'Cyber-Bombing ISIS: Why Disclose What is Better Kept Secret?', *Global Affairs*, Vol. 3, No. 2 (2017), pp. 125–37.

Johnson, Keith, 'Putin's Mediterranean Power Play in Syria', *Foreign Policy*, 2 October 2015, https://foreignpolicy.com/2015/10/02/putins-mediterranean-power-play-in-syria-navy-tartus-fleet/

Jones, Seth, *In the Graveyard of Empires: America's War in Afghanistan* (New York: Norton, 2009).

Keatinge, Tom, 'The Importance of Financing in Enabling and Sustaining the Conflict in Syria (and Beyond)', *Perspectives on Terrorism*, Vol. 8, No. 4 (2014), pp. 53–61.

Kilcullen, David, *Blood Year: Islamic State and the Failures of the War on Terror* (London: Hurst, 2016).

Krieg, Andreas, 'Externalizing the Burden of War: The Obama Doctrine and US Foreign Policy in the Middle East', *International Affairs*, Vol. 92, No. 1 (2016), pp. 97–113.

Lister, Charles, *The Syrian Jihad: Al-Qaeda, the Islamic State and the Evolution of an Insurgency* (London: Hurst, 2015).

Lister, Tim, 'A Frontline Report: The Ground War Against the Islamic State', *CTC Sentinel*, Vol. 8, Issue 11 (November/December 2015), https://ctc.usma.edu/a-frontline-report-the-ground-war-against-the-islamic-state/

Malkesian, Carter, *War Comes to Garmser* (London: Hurst, 2016).

McCants, Will, *The ISIS Apocalypse: The History, Strategy, and Doomsday Vision of the Islamic State* (New York: St. Martin's Press, 2015).

Moaveni, Azadeh, *Guest House for Young Widows: Among the Women of ISIS* (London: Scribe, 2019).

Mumford, Andrew, *Proxy Warfare* (Cambridge: Polity, 2013).

Mumford, Andrew, 'Proxy Warfare and the Future of Conflict', *RUSI Journal*, Vol. 158, No. 2 (2013), pp. 40–46.

Mumford, Andrew, *Counter-Insurgency Warfare and the Anglo-American Alliance: The 'Special Relationship' on the Rocks* (Washington, DC: Georgetown University Press, 2017).

Napoleoni, Loretta, *Merchants of Men: How Kidnapping, Ransom and Trafficking Fund Terrorism and ISIS* (London: Atlantic Books, 2018).

Neumann, Peter R., *Radicalized: New Jihadists and the Threat to the West* (London: I.B. Tauris, 2016).

Neumann, Peter R., *Bluster: Donald Trump's War on Terror* (London: Hurst, 2019).

Ohlers, C. Alexander, 'Operation Inherent Resolve and the Islamic State: Assessing "Aggressive Containment"', *Orbis*, Vol. 61, No. 2 (2017), pp. 195–211.

Phillips, Christopher, *The Battle for Syria: International Rivalry in the New Middle East* (New Haven, CT: Yale University Press, 2016).

Renz, Bettina, *Russia's Military Revival* (Cambridge: Polity, 2018).

Rhodes, Ben, *The World As It Is: Inside Obama's White House* (London: Bodley Head, 2018).

Ricks, Thomas, *Fiasco: The American Military Adventure in Iraq* (London: Penguin, 2006).

Ricks, Thomas, *The Gamble: General David Petraeus and the American Military Adventure in Iraq* (New York: Allen Lane, 2009).

Robbins, James S., 'Fighting the Islamic State: The US Scorecard', *Journal of International Security Studies*, No. 30 (Winter 2016), http://www.securityaffairs.org/issues/number-30/fighting-the-islamic-state-us-scorecard

Robinson, Linda, *Tell Me How This Ends: General David Petraeus and the Search for a Way Out of Iraq* (New York: Public Affairs, 2008).

Ryder, Nicholas, 'Out With the Old and . . . In with the Old? A Critical Review of the Financial War on Terrorism on the Islamic State of Iraq and the Levant', *Studies in Conflict and Terrorism*, Vol. 41, No. 2 (2018), pp. 79–95.

Saideman, Stephen S., 'The Ambivalent Coalition: Doing the Least One Can Do Against the Islamic State', *Contemporary Security Policy*, Vol. 37, No. 2 (2016), pp. 289–305.

Seldon, Anthony, and Peter Snowden, *Cameron at 10: The Verdict* (London: William Collins, 2016).

Shapiro, Jacob, 'A Predictable Failure: The Political Economy of the Decline of the Islamic State', *CTC Sentinel*, Vol. 9, Issue 9 (September 2016), https://ctc.usma.edu/a-predictable-failure-the-political-economy-of-the-decline-of-the-islamic-state/

Simon, Jeffrey, *Lone Wolf Terrorism: Understanding the Growing Threat* (Buffalo, NY: Prometheus Books, 2016).

Souleimanov, Emil Aslan, and Katrina Petrtylova, 'Russia's Policy Toward the Islamic State', *Middle East Policy*, Vol. 22, No. 3 (2015), https://mepc.org/russias-policy-toward-islamic-state

Stansfield, Gareth, 'Explaining the Aims, Rise, and Impact of the Islamic
    State in Iraq and al-Sham', *The Middle East Journal*, Vol. 70, No. 1 (2016),
    pp. 146–51.

Stern, Jessica, 'Obama and Terrorism', *Foreign Affairs*, Vol. 94 (September/
    October 2015), https://www.foreignaffairs.com/articles/obama-and-
    terrorism

Stern, Jessica, and J.M. Berger, *ISIS: State of Terror* (London: William
    Collins, 2015).

Thornton, Rod, 'Problems with the Kurds as Proxies Against Islamic State:
    Insights from the Siege of Kobane', *Small Wars and Insurgencies*, Vol. 26,
    No. 6 (2015), pp. 865–85.

Tønnesen, Truls Hallberg, 'The Islamic State After the Caliphate', *Perspectives
    on Terrorism*, Vol. 13, No. 1 (2019), pp. 1–11.

Warrick, Joby, *Black Flags: The Rise of ISIS* (London: Corgi Books, 2016).

Weiss, Michael, and Hassan Hassan, *ISIS: Inside the Army of Terror* (New
    York: Regan Arts, 2015).

Whiteside, Craig, 'The Islamic State and the Return of Revolutionary
    Warfare', *Small Wars and Insurgencies*, Vol. 27, No. 5 (2016), pp. 743–76.

Williams, Brian Glyn, *Counter Jihad: America's Military Experience in
    Afghanistan, Iraq and Syria* (Philadelphia, PA: University of
    Pennsylvania Press, 2017).

Wolff, Michael, *Fire and Fury: Inside the Trump White House* (London:
    Little, Brown, 2018).

Work, J. Patrick, 'Fighting the Islamic State By, With and Through', *Joint
    Forces Quarterly*, Vol. 89, No. 2 (2018), pp. 56–62.

## Media sources

Ackerman, Spencer, 'US has trained only "four or five" Syrian fighters
    against ISIS, top general testifies', *The Guardian*, 16 September 2015,
    https://www.theguardian.com/us-news/2015/sep/16/us-military-syrian-
    isis-fighters

Ahmad, Aziz, 'Undefeated, ISIS is back in Iraq', *The New York Review of
    Books blog*, 13 February 2019, https://www.nybooks.com/daily/2019/02/
    13/undefeated-isis-is-back-in-iraq/

Allen, John R., 'I was special envoy to fight the Islamic State: Our gains are now at risk', *The Washington Post*, 3 January 2019, https://www. washingtonpost.com/opinions/i-was-special-envoy-to-fight-the-islamic-state-trump-could-unravel-our-gains/2019/01/03/2339f1a4-0ebe-11e9-84fc-d58c33d6c8c7_story.html?noredirect=on&utm_term= .90099ff98b23

Associated Press, 'Obama vows not to relent against ISIS, "a bunch of killers with good social media"', *The Guardian*, 22 November 2015, https://www. theguardian.com/us-news/2015/nov/22/obama-addresses-isis-social-media-power

Associated Press, 'Russia says tens of thousands of its troops fought in Syria', 22 August 2018, https://www.apnews.com/ f787223e4fee4946be853662505e95c4

Associated Press, 'US-led coalition: 1,257 civilians killed in airstrikes against ISIS', *Air Force Times*, 28 March 2019, https://www.airforcetimes.com/ flashpoints/2019/03/29/us-led-coalition-1257-civilians-killed-in-airstrikes-against-isis/?utm_expid=.jFR93cgdTFyMrWXdYEtvgA.1 &utm_referrer=https%3A%2F%2Fwww.google.com%2F#jwvideo

Baker, Peter, 'A coalition in which some do more than others to fight ISIS', *The New York Times*, 29 November 2015, https://www.nytimes.com/ 2015/11/30/us/politics/a-coalition-in-which-some-do-more-than-others-to-fight-isis.html

Baker, Peter, Helene Cooper, and David E. Sanger, 'Obama sends Special Operations Forces to help fight ISIS in Syria', *The New York Times*, 30 October 2015, https://www.nytimes.com/2015/10/31/ world/obama-will-send-forces-to-syria-to-help-fight-the-islamic-state.html

Barnard, Anne, and Thomas Erdbrink, 'ISIS makes gains in Syria territory bombed by Russia', *The New York Times*, 9 October 2015, https://www. nytimes.com/2015/10/10/world/middleeast/hussein-hamedani-iran-general-killed-in-syria.html

Bauke, Nicole, 'US, coalition form new advisory team to better train, assist Iraqi air force', *Air Force Times*, 5 February 2018, https://www. airforcetimes.com/flashpoints/2018/02/05/us-coalition-form-new-advisory-team-to-better-train-assist-iraqi-air-force/

BBC News, 'US and UK suspend non-lethal aid for Syria rebels', 11 December 2013, http://www.bbc.co.uk/news/world-middle-east-25331241

BBC News, 'How ISIS is spreading its message online', 19 June 2014, https://www.bbc.co.uk/news/world-middle-east-27912569

BBC News, 'Germany to supply arms to Kurds fighting IS in Iraq', 1 September 2014, https://www.bbc.co.uk/news/world-europe-29012159

BBC News, 'Islamic State: US probes "stray Syria air drop" in IS video', 22 October 2014, http://www.bbc.co.uk/news/world-middle-east-29715044

BBC News, 'Qatar officials dismiss IS funding claims', 27 October 2014, http://www.bbc.co.uk/news/world-middle-east-29782291

BBC News, 'Assad says Syria is informed on anti-IS air campaign', 10 February 2015, http://www.bbc.co.uk/news/world-middle-east-31312414

BBC News, 'UK to give military training to "moderate Syria forces"', 26 March 2015, http://www.bbc.co.uk/news/uk-32064130

BBC News, 'US campaign against Islamic State in Syria "intensifying"', 7 July 2015, http://www.bbc.co.uk/news/world-middle-east-33418021

BBC News, 'Turkey's downing of Russian warplane – what we know', 1 December 2015, https://www.bbc.co.uk/news/world-middle-east-34912581

BBC News, 'Islamic State group "lost quarter of territory" in 2016', 19 January 2017, http://www.bbc.co.uk/news/world-middle-east-38641509

BBC News, 'Military boss defends RAF bombings of IS', 8 June 2018, https://www.bbc.co.uk/news/uk-44404828

BBC News, 'Syria conflict: US officials withdraw troops after IS "defeat"', 19 December 2018, https://www.bbc.co.uk/news/world-middle-east-46623617

BBC News, 'Two British soldiers injured in Islamic State attack in Syria', 6 January 2019, https://www.bbc.co.uk/news/uk-46772412

BBC News, 'US to expel last Iranian boot from Syria – Pompeo', 10 January 2019, https://www.bbc.co.uk/news/world-middle-east-46828810

BBC News, 'US-backed Syrian fighters "overrun IS encampment"', 19 March 2019, https://www.bbc.co.uk/news/world-middle-east-47628209

BBC News, 'Abu Bakr al-Baghdadi: what his death means for IS in Syria', 27 October 2019, https://www.bbc.co.uk/news/world-middle-east-50199437

Bender, Brian, 'Pentagon halts fight against ISIS in Iraq amid new threats to bases', *Politico*, 5 January 2020, https://www.politico.com/news/2020/01/05/pentagon-halts-fight-isis-iraq-bases-094140

Berger, J.M., 'How ISIS Games Twitter', *The Atlantic,* 16 June 2014, https://www.theatlantic.com/international/archive/2014/06/isis-iraq-twitter-social-media-strategy/372856/

Berger, J.M., 'Barack Obama still misunderestimates ISIL', *Politico*, 22 May 2015, https://www.politico.com/magazine/story/2015/05/barack-obama-still-misunderestimates-isil-118204

Bew, John, and Shiraz Maher, 'Syria's World War', *New Statesman*, 11 April 2018, https://www.newstatesman.com/world/middle-east/2018/04/syria-assad-trump-war-britain-us-strike-russia

Borger, Julian, 'Defense Secretary James Mattis resigns and points to differences with Trump', *The Guardian*, 21 December 2018, https://www.theguardian.com/us-news/2018/dec/20/jim-mattis-defense-secretary-retires-trump

Burke, Jason, 'Rise and fall of ISIS: its dream of a caliphate is over, so what now?', *The Guardian*, 21 October 2017, https://www.theguardian.com/world/2017/oct/21/isis-caliphate-islamic-state-raqqa-iraq-islamist

Callimachi, Rukmini, and Eric Schmitt, 'Splitting with Trump over Syria, American leading ISIS fight steps down', *The New York Times*, 22 December 2018, https://www.nytimes.com/2018/12/22/world/brett-mcgurk-isis-resign.html

Chmaytelli, Maher, and Ahmed Aboulenein, 'Iraq declares final victory over Islamic State', *Reuters*, 9 December 2017, https://www.reuters.com/article/us-mideast-crisis-iraq-islamicstate/iraq-declares-final-victory-over-islamic-state-idUSKBN1E30B9

Chulov, Martin, 'Amid the bloody chaos of Syria, Iran's game plan is laid bare: a path to the sea', *The Observer*, 9 October 2016, https://www.theguardian.com/world/2016/oct/08/iran-iraq-syria-isis-land-corridor

Chulov, Martin, and Mohammed Rasool, 'Isis founding member confirmed by spies as group's new leader', *The Guardian*, 20 January 2020, https://www.theguardian.com/world/2020/jan/20/isis-leader-confirmed-amir-mohammed-abdul-rahman-al-mawli-al-salbi

Clemons, Steve, '"Thank God for the Saudis": ISIS, Iraq, and the lessons of blowback', *The Atlantic*, 23 June 2014, http://theatlantic.com/international/archive/2014/06/isis-saudi-arabia-iraq-syria-bandar/373181

Cobain, Ian, Alice Ross, Rob Evans, and Mona Mahmood, 'How Britain funds the "propaganda war" against ISIS in Syria', *The Guardian*, 3 May 2016, http://www.theguardian.com/world/2016/may/03/how-britain-funds-the-propaganda-war-against-isis-in-syria

Cooper, Helene, 'Obama requests money to train "appropriately vetted" Syrian rebels', *The New York Times*, 26 June 2014, www.nytimes.com/2014/06/27/world/middleeast/obama-seeks-500-million-to-train-and-equip-syrian-opposition.html

Cooper, Helene, and Alissa J. Rubin, 'The US seemed to be leaving Iraq but it was all an 'honest mistake'', *New York Times*, 6 January 2020, https://www.nytimes.com/2020/01/06/world/middleeast/iran-letter-withdrawal-iraq.html

Cooper, Helene, and Eric Schmitt, 'ISIS official killed in US raid in Syria, Pentagon says', *The New York Times*, 16 May 2015, https://www.nytimes.com/2015/05/17/world/middleeast/abu-sayyaf-isis-commander-killed-by-us-forces-pentagon-says.html

El-Ghobashy, Tamir, Maria Abi-Habib, and Benoit Faucon, 'France directs kills of French fighters in ISIS', *Wall Street Journal*, 30 May 2017, https://www.wsj.com/articles/frances-special-forces-hunt-french-militants-fighting-for-islamic-state-1496090116

Engel, Richard, and Kennett Werner, 'White House chaos jeopardizes war on ISIS, US commanders warn', NBC News, 20 March 2018, https://www.nbcnews.com/news/world/white-house-chaos-jeopardizes-war-isis-u-s-commanders-warn-n859966

Ensor, Josie, 'US Special Forces carry out secret ground raid against ISIL in Syria, "killing at least 25 jihadists"', *The Telegraph*, 9 January 2017, https://www.telegraph.co.uk/news/2017/01/09/us-special-forces-carry-ground-raid-against-isil/

Farmer, Ben, 'SAS "took part in Abu Sayyaf ISIL raid in Syria"', *The Telegraph*, 9 August 2015, https://www.telegraph.co.uk/news/uknews/defence/11793011/SAS-took-part-in-Abu-Sayyaf-Isil-raid-in-Syria.html

Filkins, Dexter, 'The dangers posed by the killing of Qassem Suleimani', *The New Yorker*, 3 January 2020, https://www.newyorker.com/news/daily-comment/the-dangers-posed-by-the-killing-of-qassem-suleimani

Friedman, Thomas L., 'Obama on the world', *The New York Times*, 8 August 2014, https://www.nytimes.com/2014/08/09/opinion/president-obama-thomas-l-friedman-iraq-and-world-affairs.html

Galbraith, Peter W., 'The betrayal of the Kurds', *The New York Review of Books*, 21 November 2019, https://www.nybooks.com/articles/2019/11/21/betrayal-of-the-kurds/

Garland, Chad, 'US special operations troops turn to drones to remotely advise Iraqis', *Stars and Stripes*, 4 May 2020, https://www.stripes.com/news/middle-east/us-special-operations-troops-turn-to-drones-to-remotely-advise-iraqis-1.628337

Gibbons-Neff, Thomas, 'The American intervention against ISIS is just another chapter in an endless war', *The New York Times Magazine*, 29 March 2019, https://www.nytimes.com/2019/03/29/magazine/isis-syria-defeat.html

Gibbons-Neff, Thomas, and Eric Schmitt, 'Pentagon considers using Special Operations Forces to continue missions in Syria', *The New York Times*, 21 December 2018, https://www.nytimes.com/2018/12/21/us/politics/pentagon-syria-iraq-kurds.html

Gidda, Mirren, 'Cash crunch in the Caliphate', *Newsweek*, 2 October 2015, https://www.newsweek.com/2015/10/02/isis-are-facing-cash-crunch-caliphate-375490.html

Giglio, Mike, 'America is in a proxy war with itself in Syria', *Buzzfeed News*, 20 February 2016, http://www.buzzfeed.com/mikegiglio/america-is-now-fighting-a-proxy-war-with-itself-in-syria?htm_term=.pya4DXoBb#.gkrErY4k2

Goldberg, Jeffrey, 'The Obama doctrine', *The Atlantic*, April 2016, https://www.theatlantic.com/magazine/archive/2016/04/the-obama-doctrine/471525/

Hassan, Falih, and Rod Nordland, 'Battered ISIS keeps grip on last piece of territory for over a year', *The New York Times*, 9 December 2018, https://www.nytimes.com/2018/12/09/world/middleeast/isis-territory-syria-iraq.html

Hassan, Hassan, 'Iran won't surrender militias that conduct Assad's war', *The National*, 10 January 2016, http://www.thenational.ae/opinion/comment/iran-wont-surrender-militias-that-conduct-assads-war

Hennigan, W.J., '"I was not consulted": Top US general left out of Syria withdrawal decision', *TIME Magazine*, 5 February 2019, https://time.com/5521419/syria-withdrawal-donald-trump-joseph-votel/

Ignatius, David, 'Foreign nations' proxy war in Syria creates chaos', *The Washington Post*, 2 October 2014, http://www.washingtonpost.com/opinions/david-ignatius-foreign-nations-proxy-war-creates-syrian-chaos/2014/10/02/061fb50c-4a7a-11e4-a046-120a8a855cca_story.html

Kenner, David, 'All ISIS has left is money: lots of it', *The Atlantic*, 24 March 2019, https://www.theatlantic.com/international/archive/2019/03/isis-caliphate-money-territory/584911/

Khan, Azmat, and Anand Gopal, 'The uncounted', *The New York Times Magazine*, 16 November 2017, https://www.nytimes.com/interactive/2017/11/16/magazine/uncounted-civilian-casualties-iraq-airstrikes.html

Knight, Michael, 'How the Islamic State feeds on coronavirus', *Politico*, 8 April 2020, https://www.politico.com/news/magazine/2020/04/08/how-the-islamic-state-feeds-on-coronavirus-175192

Lamothe, Dan, 'How the Pentagon's cyber offensive against ISIS could shape the future for elite US forces', *The Washington Post*, 16 December 2017, https://www.washingtonpost.com/news/checkpoint/wp/2017/12/16/how-the-pentagons-cyber-offensive-against-isis-could-shape-the-future-for-elite-u-s-forces/?utm_term=.0975443aa419

Letsch, Constanze, 'Turkey denies new deal reached to open airbases to US in fight against ISIS', *The Guardian*, 13 October 2014, https://www.theguardian.com/world/2014/oct/13/turkey-denies-agreement-open-air-bases-us-isis

Lister, Charles, and William F. Wechsler, 'Trump has big plans for Syria, but he has no real strategy', *Politico*, 20 January 2018, https://www.politico.com/magazine/story/2018/01/30/donald-trump-syria-strategy-216551

Loveluck, Louisa, 'Turkish president threatens to "drown" US-backed force in Syria', *The Washington Post*, 15 January 2018, https://www.washingtonpost.com/world/turkish-president-threatens-todrown-us-backed-force-in-syria/2018/01/15/e7789850-f9e7-11e7-b832-8c26844b74fb_story.html

Malyasov, Dylan, 'French military announces start of Iraq withdrawal',
*Defence Blog*, 7 April 2019, https://defence-blog.com/army/french-
military-announces-start-of-iraq-withdrawal.html

Mazzetti, Mark, and Matt Apuzzo, 'US relies heavily on Saudi money to
support Syrian rebels', *The New York Times*, 23 January 2016, https://
www.nytimes.com/2016/01/24/world/middleeast/us-relies-heavily-on-
saudi-money-to-support-syrian-rebels.html

Mazzetti, Mark, Anne Barnard, and Eric Schmitt, 'Military success in Syria
gives Putin upper hand in US proxy war', *The New York Times*, 6 August
2016, http://www.nytimes.com/2016/08/07/world/middleeast/military-
syria-putin-us-proxy-war.html

Mazzetti, Mark, Adam Goldman, and Michael S. Schmidt, 'Behind the
sudden death of a $1billion secret CIA war in Syria', *New York Times*,
2 August 2017, https://www.nytimes.com/2017/08/02/world/middleeast/
cia-syria-rebel-arm-train-trump.html

McCarthy, Niall, 'The cost of the air war against ISIS has reached $11
billion', *Forbes*, 1 February 2017, https://www.forbes.com/sites/
niallmccarthy/2017/02/01/the-cost-of-the-air-war-against-isis-has-
reached-11-billion-infographic/#33f8b2bcb120

McLeary, Paul, 'Russia winning info & electronic war in Syria, US and UK
generals warn', *Breaking Defense*, 9 October 2018, https://
breakingdefense.com/2018/10/russia-winning-information-electronic-
war-over-syria-us-uk-generals-warn/

Mehta, Aaron, 'Carter again slams anti-ISIS partners on lack of assistance',
*Defense News*, 2 February 2016, https://www.defensenews.com/
pentagon/2016/02/02/carter-again-slams-anti-isis-partners-on-lack-of-
assistance/

Miller, Greg, 'CIA ramping up covert training program for moderate Syrian
rebels', *The Washington Post*, 2 October 2013, https://www.
washingtonpost.com/world/national-security/cia-ramping-up-covert-
training-program-for-moderate-syrian-rebels/2013/10/02/a0bba084-
2af6-11e3-8ade-a1f23cda135e_story.html?utm_term=.3ab61eed5d2d

Miller, Greg, 'US launches secret drone campaign to hunt Islamic State
leaders', *The Washington Post*, 1 September 2015, https://www.
washingtonpost.com/world/national-security/us-launches-secret-drone-

campaign-to-hunt-islamic-state-leaders-in-syria/2015/09/01/723b3e04-
5033-11e5-933e-7d06c647a395_story.html

Nakashima, Ellen, 'US military cyber operation to attack ISIS last year
sparked heated debate over alerting allies', *The Washington Post*, 9 May
2017, https://www.washingtonpost.com/world/national-security/
us-military-cyber-operation-to-attack-isis-last-year-sparked-heated-
debate-over-alerting-allies/2017/05/08/93a120a2-30d5-11e7-9dec-
764dc781686f_story.html?utm_term=.ca1701f8708c

Naylor, Hugh, 'Iranian media is revealing that scores of the country's fighters
are dying in Syria', *The Washington Post*, 27 November 2015, https://www.
washingtonpost.com/world/iranian-media-is-revealing-that-scores-of-
the-countrys-fighters-are-dying-in-syria/2015/11/27/294deb02-8ca0-
11e5-934c-a369c80822c2_story.html

NBC News, 'How to beat ISIS: blow up the money', 29 April 2016, https://
www.nbcnews.com/storyline/isis-terror/how-beat-isis-blow-money-
n564956

Ozkan, Mert, and Ellen Francis, 'Airstrikes pound Syria's Afrin as Turkey
launches "Operation Olive Branch"', *Reuters*, 20 January 2018, https://
uk.reuters.com/article/uk-mideast-crisis-syria-turkey/airstrikes-pound-
syrias-afrin-as-turkey-launches-operation-olive-branch-
idUKKBN1F90RS

Parkinson, Joe, and Dion Nissenbaum, 'US allies training Kurds on using
sophisticated weaponry against Islamic State', *The Wall Street Journal*,
21 September 2014, http://www.wsj.com/articles/U-S-allies -training-
kurds-on-using-islamic-state-1411339625

Pawlyk, Oriana, 'ISIS kill missions: 1 in 5 drone flights includes a missile
strike', *Air Force Times*, 30 March 2016, https://www.airforcetimes.com/
news/your-air-force/2016/03/30/isis-kill-missions-1-in-5-drone-flights-
includes-a-missile-strike/

Pffaf, C. Anthony, and Patrick Granfield, 'How (not) to fight proxy wars', *The
National Interest*, 27 March 2018, https://nationalinterest.org/feature/
how-not-fight-proxy-wars-25102

Remnick, David, 'Going the distance', *The New Yorker*, 27 January 2014,
www.newyorker.com/magazine/2014/01/27/going-the-distance-david-
remnick

Reuters, 'Exclusive: US commanders recommend letting Kurdish fighters in Syria keep weapons', 28 December 2018, https://uk.reuters.com/article/uk-mideast-crisis-syria-usa-exclusive/exclusive-u-s-commanders-recommend-letting-kurdish-fighters-in-syria-keep-weapons-idUKKCN1OR1OH

Rogin, Josh, 'Trump undermines his entire national security team on Syria', *The Washington Post*, 19 December 2018, https://www.washingtonpost.com/opinions/2018/12/19/trump-undermines-his-entire-national-security-team-syria/

Rubin, Alissa J., and Anne Barnard, 'France strikes ISIS targets in Syria in retaliation for attacks', *The New York Times*, 15 November 2015, https://www.nytimes.com/2015/11/16/world/europe/paris-terror-attack.html

Ruthven, Malise, 'How to understand ISIS', *The New York Review of Books*, 23 June 2016, https://www.nybooks.com/articles/2016/06/23/how-to-understand-isis/

Sabbagh, Dan, 'Anti-ISIS coalition suspends operations as Iraqi MPs vote to expel US troops', *The Guardian*, 5 January 2020, https://www.theguardian.com/world/2020/jan/05/anti-isis-coalition-suspends-operations-as-iraqi-mps-vote-to-expel-us-troops

Sanger, David E., 'US cyberattacks target ISIS in a new line of combat', *The New York Times*, 24 April 2016, https://www.nytimes.com/2016/04/25/us/politics/us-directs-cyberweapons-at-isis-for-first-time.html

Sanger, David E., and Julian E. Barnes, 'On North Korea and Iran, intelligence chiefs contradict Trump', *The New York Times*, 29 January 2019, https://www.nytimes.com/2019/01/29/us/politics/kim-jong-trump.html

Scales, Robert H., 'The only way to defeat the Islamic State', *The Washington Post*, 5 September 2014, https://www.washingtonpost.com/opinions/the-only-way-to-defeat-the-islamic-state/2014/09/05/4b2d7bd4-3459-11e4-a723-fa3895a25d02_story.html

Schake, Kori, 'Rex Tillerson's Syria policy is sensible – but it's fanciful', *The Atlantic*, 18 January 2018, https://www.theatlantic.com/international/archive/2018/01/tillerson-syria-stanford/550853/

Schmitt, Eric, and Michael Gordon, 'US sees risks in assisting a compromised Iraqi force', *The New York Times*, 14 July 2014, https://

www.nytimes.com/2014/07/14/world/middleeast/us-sees-risks-in-assisting-a-compromised-iraqi-force.html

Schmitt, Eric, and Ben Hubbard, 'US revamping rebel force fighting ISIS in Syria', *The New York Times*, 6 September 2015, http://www.nytimes.com/2015/09/07/world/middleeast/us-to-revamp-training-program-to-fight-isis.html

Schogol, Jeff, 'Mattis says Syria policy has not changed after White House changes Syria policy', *Task and Purpose*, 24 September 2018, https://taskandpurpose.com/news/mattis-says-no-syria-policy-changes

Shaheen, Kareem, Shaun Walker, Julian Borger, and David Smith, 'Putin condemns Turkey after Russian warplane downed near Syria border', *The Guardian*, 24 November 2015, https://www.theguardian.com/world/2015/nov/24/turkey-shoots-down-jet-near-border-with-syria

Sherlock, Ruth, 'Syrian rebels armed and trained by US surrendered to al-Qaeda', *The Telegraph*, 2 November 2014, http://www.telegraph.co.uk/news/worldnews/middleeast/syria/11203825/Syrian-rebels-armed-and-trained-by-US-surrender-to-al-Qaeda.html

Sly, Liz, 'Did US weapons supplied to Syrian rebels draw Russia into the conflict?', *The Washington Post*, 11 October 2015, https://www.washingtonpost.com/world/did-us-weapons-supplied-to-syrian-rebels-draw-russia-into-the-conflict/2015/10/11/268ce566-6dfc-11e5-91eb-27ad15c2b723_story.html

Solomon, Jay, and Carol E. Lee, 'Iran's Ayatollah sends new letter to Obama amid nuclear talks', *The Wall Street Journal*, 13 February 2015, https://www.wsj.com/articles/irans-ayatollah-sends-new-letter-to-obama-amid-nuclear-talks-1423872638

Steele, Jonathan, 'Putin in Syria', *London Review of Books*, 21 April 2016, https://www.lrb.co.uk/the-paper/v38/n08/jonathan-steele/putin-in-syria

Stein, Jeff, 'Inside the CIA's Syrian rebels vetting machine', *Newsweek*, 21 November 2014, https://www.newsweek.com/2014/11/21/moderate-rebels-please-raise-your-hands-283449.html

Stevenson, Tom, 'How to run a Caliphate', *London Review of Books*, 20 June 2019, https://www.lrb.co.uk/the-paper/v41/n12/tom-stevenson/how-to-run-a-caliphate

Taub, Ben, 'Iraq's post-ISIS campaign of revenge', *The New Yorker*, December 2018, https://www.newyorker.com/magazine/2018/12/24/iraqs-post-isis-campaign-of-revenge

Temple-Raston, Dina, 'How the US hacked ISIS', *NPR*, 26 September 2019, https://www.npr.org/2019/09/26/763545811/how-the-u-s-hacked-isis

*The Economist*, 'Decapitated, not defeated', 2 November 2019, https://www.economist.com/middle-east-and-africa/2019/11/02/islamic-state-after-the-death-of-abu-bakr-al-baghdadi

Tilghman, Andrew, 'US advisory mission in Iraq remains limited in scope', *Military Times*, 20 October 2014, https://www.militarytimes.com/2014/10/20/u-s-advisory-mission-in-iraq-remains-limited-in-scope-and-impact/

Torbati, Yeganelu, and Brett Wolf, 'In taking economic war to Islamic State, US developing new tools', *Reuters*, 24 November 2015, https://www.reuters.com/article/us-france-shooting-usa-sanctions-insight/in-taking-economic-war-to-islamic-state-u-s-developing-new-tools-idUSKBN0T D0BJ20151124?feedType=RSS&feedName=worldNews

Walker, Shaun, Kareem Shaheen, Martin Chulov, Spencer Ackerman, and Julian Borger, 'US accuses Russia of "throwing gasoline on the fire" of Syrian civil war', *The Guardian*, 1 October 2015, https://www.theguardian.com/world/2015/sep/30/russia-launches-first-airstrikes-against-targets-in-syria-says-us

Warrick, Joby, 'Inside the economic war against the Islamic State', *The Washington Post*, 31 December 2016, https://www.washingtonpost.com/world/national-security/take-them-back-to-the-19th-century-inside-the-economic-war-against-the-islamic-state/2016/12/30/5f91f514-ceb7-11e6-a747-d03044780a02_story.html

Warrick, Joby, 'Retreating ISIS army smuggled a fortune in cash and gold out of Iraq and Syria', *The Washington Post*, 21 December 2018, https://www.washingtonpost.com/world/national-security/retreating-isis-army-smuggled-a-fortune-in-cash-and-gold-out-of-iraq-and-syria/2018/12/21/95087ffc-054b-11e9-9122-82e98f91ee6f_story.html

Weaver, Mary Anne, 'The short, violent life of Abu Musab al-Zarqawi', *The Atlantic*, July/August 2006, https://www.theatlantic.com/magazine/

archive/2006/07/the-short-violent-life-of-abu-musab-al-zarqawi/
304983/

Whittle, Richard, 'The unprecedented way America is fighting ISIS', *The New York Post*, 28 May 2016, https://nypost.com/2016/05/28/a-surreal-day-inside-our-war-against-isis/

Wintour, Patrick, 'Putin brings Iran and Turkey together in bold Syria peace plan', *The Guardian*, 22 November 2017, https://www.theguardian.com/world/2017/nov/22/iranian-and-turkish-leaders-arrive-in-russia-for-syria-talks-with-putin

Wood, Graeme, 'What ISIS really wants', *The Atlantic*, March 2015, http://www.theatlantic.com/features/archive/2015/02/what-isis-really-wants/384980

Wright, Robin, 'The ignominious end of the ISIS caliphate', *The New Yorker*, 17 October 2017, https://www.newyorker.com/news/news-desk/the-ignominious-end-of-the-isis-caliphate

Wright, Robin, 'The breathtaking unravelling of the Middle East after Qassem Suleimani's death', *The New Yorker*, 6 January 2020, https://www.newyorker.com/news/our-columnists/the-breathtaking-unravelling-of-the-middle-east-after-suleimanis-death

## Thinktank reports

Airwars, 'Limited Accountability: A Transparency Audit of the Coalition Air War Against So-Called Islamic State' (Oxford: Oxford Research Group, December 2016), https://airwars.org/report/limited-accountability-a-transparency-audit-of-the-coalition-air-war-against-so-called-islamic-state/

Australian Strategic Policy Institute (APSI), 'Strike from the Air: The First 100 Days of the Campaign Against ISIL' (December 2014), https://www.aspi.org.au/report/strike-air-first-100-days-campaign-against-isil

Carter, Ash, 'A Lasting Defeat: The Campaign to Destroy ISIS', Belfer Center special report (October 2017), https://www.belfercenter.org/LastingDefeat

Center for a New American Security (CNAS), 'Defeating the Islamic State: A Bottom-Up Approach' (June 2016), https://www.cnas.org/publications/reports/defeating-the-islamic-state-a-bottom-up-approach

Conflict Armament Research, 'Weapons of the Islamic State' (December 2017), https://www.conflictarm.com/weapons-of-the-islamic-state/

Cordesman, Anthony H., 'The Islamic State War: No Clear US Strategy', Center for Strategic and International Studies (CSIS) research paper (November 2014), https://www.csis.org/analysis/islamic-state-war-no-clear-us-strategy

Danish Institute for International Studies policy brief, 'A Difficult Balancing Act: Backing the Kurds in the Fight Against IS in Iraq and Syria' (November 2014), https://pure.diis.dk/ws/files/632411/diis_pb_backing_the_kurds_print.pdf

Eyal, Jonathan, and Elizabeth Quintana (eds.), 'Inherently Unresolved: The Military Operation Against ISIS', *RUSI Occasional Paper* (London: RUSI, 2015), https://rusi.org/publication/occasional-papers/inherently-unresolved-military-operation-against-isis

Fidler, David P., 'Terrorism, the Internet, and Islamic State's Defeat: It's Over But It's Not Over Yet', *Council on Foreign Relations blog* (28 November 2017), https://www.cfr.org/blog/terrorism-internet-and-islamic-states-defeat-its-over-its-not-over

International Crisis Group, 'Arming Iraq's Kurds: Fighting IS, Inviting Conflict', *Middle East Report*, No. 158 (12 May 2015), https://www.crisisgroup.org/middle-east-north-africa/gulf-and-arabian-peninsula/iraq/arming-iraq-s-kurds-fighting-inviting-conflict

International Crisis Group, 'Contending with ISIS in the Time of Coronavirus' (31 March 2020), https://www.crisisgroup.org/global/contending-isis-time-coronavirus

Jones, Seth G. (ed.), 'Moscow's War in Syria' (Washington, DC: Center for Strategic and International Studies, May 2020), https://www.csis.org/analysis/moscows-war-syria

Jonsson, Michael, 'Funding the Islamic State: Sources of Revenue, Financing Requirements and Long-Term Vulnerabilities to Counter Measures', Swedish Defence Research Agency, Asia Security Briefing (December 2015), https://www.foi.se/download/18.7fd35d7f166c56ebe0bc0e8/1542369070574/Funding-the-Islamic-State_FOI-Memo-5525.pdf

Kasapoglu, Can, and Sinan Ulgen, 'Operation Olive Branch: A Political-Military Assessment', Centre for Economics and Foreign Policy Studies

(EDAM) occasional paper (January 2018), https://edam.org.tr/en/
operation-olive-branch-a-political-military-assessment/

Keatinge, Tom, 'Defeating ISIS: How Financial Liabilities Will Undo the
Jihadists', *RUSI Commentary blog* (27 October 2014), https://rusi.org/
commentary/defeating-isis-how-financial-liabilities-will-undo-
jihadists

Khatib, Lina, and Lina Sinjab, 'Syria's Transactional State: How the Conflict
Changed the Syrian State's Exercise of Power', Chatham House research
paper (London: Chatham House, October 2018), https://www.
chathamhouse.org/publication/syrias-transactional-state-how-conflict-
changed-syrian-states-exercise-power

Levitt, Matthew, 'Countering ISIL Financing: A Realistic Assessment',
Washington Institute for Near East Policy briefing note (2 February
2015), https://www.washingtoninstitute.org/uploads/Documents/other/
LevittStatement20150202-v3.pdf

Lister, Charles, 'Profiling the Islamic State' (Washington, DC: Brookings
Institute, December 2014), https://www.brookings.edu/research/
profiling-the-islamic-state/

Lister, Charles, 'The Free Syrian Army: A Decentralized Insurgent Brand',
Brookings Project on US Relations with the Islamic World Analysis
Paper #26 (November 2016), https://www.brookings.edu/research/
the-free-syrian-army-a-decentralized-insurgent-brand/

Martin, Patrick, and Christopher Kozak, 'The Pitfalls of Relying on Kurdish
Forces in Counter ISIS' (Washington, DC: Institute for the Study of War,
February 2016), http://www.understandingwar.org/backgrounder/
pitfalls-relying-kurdish-forces-counter-isis-0

Pollack, Kenneth M., 'Iraq Situation Report, Part I: The Military Campaign
Against ISIS' (Washington, DC: Brookings Institute, 28 March 2016),
https://www.brookings.edu/blog/markaz/2016/03/28/iraq-situation-
report-part-i-the-military-campaign-against-isis/

RAND Corporation, 'Financial Futures of the Islamic State of Iraq and the
Levant' (Santa Monica, CA: RAND, 2017), https://www.rand.org/pubs/
conf_proceedings/CF361.html

Robinson, Linda, 'Assessment of the Politico-Military Campaign to Counter
ISIL and Options for Adaptation', RAND Corporation report (Santa

Monica, CA: RAND, 2016), https://www.rand.org/pubs/research_
reports/RR1290.html

Soufan Center, 'Iran's Playbook: Deconstructing Tehran's Regional Strategy'
(Washington, DC, May 2019), https://thesoufancenter.org/research/
irans-playbook-deconstructing-tehrans-regional-strategy/

Van der Heide, Liesbeth, Charlie Winter, and Shiraz Maher, 'The Cost of
Crying Victory: Policy Implications of the Islamic State's Territorial
Collapse' (The Hague: International Centre for Counter-Terrorism
report, November 2018), https://icct.nl/publication/the-cost-of-crying-
victory-policy-implications-of-the-islamic-states-territorial-collapse/

# Index